Samsung Ga... User Guide

The 100% Unofficial Samsung Galaxy S5 User Guide

Proud owner of the Galaxy S5?

You've got the most powerful smartphone on the market. This guide will help you learn how to harness it!

By
Daniel Forrester
Author & Tech Enthusiast

Table of Contents

The Basics of the Galaxy S5

Phone Hardware Interface

The Samsung Galaxy S5 has many features which are not commonly found in competing smartphones, making it one of the most versatile and powerful phones available on the market today. This abundance of features starts before even accessing the touch screen components, with the device interface. Understanding the layout of the device interface is a very important initial step for getting the most out of your Galaxy S5.

Front

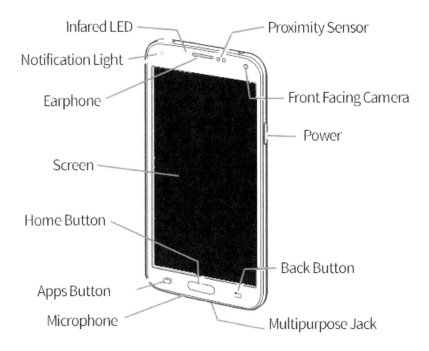

The front of your Samsung Galaxy S5 has an array of features that provide critical functions in operating your smartphone.

Home button – The home button will return you to your home screen from any other screen within your Galaxy S5. You can also use this button to safely wake your phone from sleep mode.

Apps button – The apps button will show apps that are currently open and running. Swipe apps to the left to close them if you are not in the process of using them.

Back button – The back button will return you to the previous viewing screen.

Multipurpose jack - Located on the underside of your phone, the multipurpose jack is a USB enabled connection that allows you to connect your Galaxy S5 to various devices with USB ports.

Microphone – Located on the underside of your phone, the microphone picks up and transmits your voice. The Galaxy S5 microphone is very powerful and, as such, it is not necessary to speak directly into the microphone for your voice to be audible.

Touch screen – The main pane of interaction for your Galaxy S5, the touch screen is where you will use your phone's apps and functions.

Power button – Located on the right side of your phone, the power button can be held down to power your phone on and off. It can also be pushed once, quickly, to wake your phone from sleep mode or to lock your phone when it is inactive.

Front camera – A front-facing camera for taking pictures of yourself or participating in video conferencing. Note that the front camera's resolution is significantly lower, at only 2-

megapixels, than the back camera, which has a resolution of 13-megapixels.

Proximity/Gesture sensor – The proximity/gesture sensor detects whether you are performing certain gestures and how close objects are to your phone. This is particularly useful when making a call, as the proximity sensor will lock your phone to prevent unwanted interaction with the touch screen.

Earphone – The earphone transmits audio from a phone call when you are not wearing a headset. Note that all other audio, e.g., from music or games, is transmitted via the back panel speaker.

Infrared (Ir) LED – The infrared LED is used to transmit signals when the Galaxy S5 is enabled as a universal remote.

Notification light – Flashes when the phone is performing different functions. These include phone operations, such as booting up or shutting down, and alerts about received emails or text messages.

Back

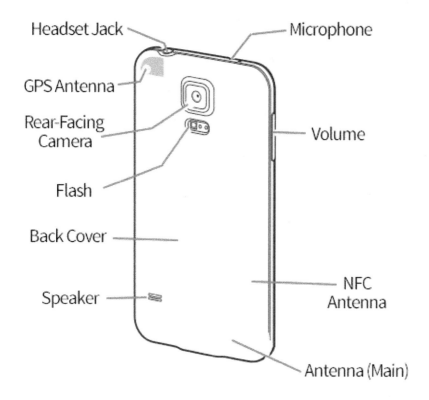

Headset Jack

Microphone

GPS Antenna

Rear-Facing Camera

Volume

Flash

Back Cover

Speaker

NFC Antenna

Antenna (Main)

Speaker – Most game and music audio will come through the speaker, as opposed to the earpiece on the front of your phone.

Main antenna – The main antenna transmits and receives signals to and from your phone. Try not to block the antenna excessively when placing calls or accessing data via the mobile network.

Back cover – The back cover of your phone can be removed to access, among other things, your phone battery and SIM card.

The Galaxy S5 will not allow normal operation of your phone until the back cover is properly put back in place.

Volume button – Located on the side of your phone, the volume button can be used to adjust the volume of calls, music, and in-app audio. Press up on the button to increase the volume, and down to decrease it.

Rear camera – The rear camera is a high-resolution camera for taking high definition pictures and movies. At 13-megapixels, it is significantly higher quality than the front camera.

Flash – The flash can be used for taking pictures in low light. It is possible to enable and disable the flash from your camera preferences.

GPS antenna – This antenna transmits GPS data to better determine your location and locate your phone.

Headset jack – This port connects to all 1/8" jack devices, including a phone headset or third-party headphones.

Microphone – This microphone can be used for speakerphone and for giving voice commands, as opposed to the microphone located on the underside of the phone, used for phone conversations.

Startup and Initial Operation

When you first start your Samsung Galaxy S5, you will be prompted to accept a few user agreements. First, you must accept the terms of the End User License Agreement for Software.

To agree to the terms and continue, click the empty box next to the text that reads, "I understand and agree to the terms and conditions above." A green check should appear in the box.

Next, peruse the Consent to Provide Diagnostic and Usage Data box. It is not necessary to consent to allow Samsung to collect usage data from your device to use your Galaxy S5, but it helps Samsung to diagnose software users across their user base to produce valuable software updates.

If you would like to give Samsung permission to collect diagnostic and usage data from your phone, select "Yes." If not, select "No thanks." The circle next to your choice should illuminate green.

After making this decision, you should advance to the next screen, "Got Google?" Here, you will be prompted to enter the information for your Google account. Most users will know their

Google account information from their familiarity with using Gmail. If you do not have a Google account, you will be required to set one up at this stage. You must have a Google account to use your Galaxy S5, and integrating your Google account adds many benefits to your S5 experience.

If you do have an account, select "Yes" and you will proceed to the next page, where you will be asked to enter your Google account login information. This is the same information you use to access your regular Gmail or Google Apps account.

When you enter your login information, you will be asked again to consent to Google's terms of agreement. Click "Yes" at this popup, or you will not be able to proceed with using your phone. You will then proceed to the Google Services screen. Here, you have the opportunity to enable backup and restore, and location services. Both are highly recommended, backup and restore can be used to recover your device, and location services will help greatly with any map or location based apps.

You will next be prompted to enter your credit card information for the Google Play store. You can do this now, or at any time in the future, from within the Google Play store. Your phone will then synchronize your Google data, and prompt you to set up your Samsung account, your email accounts, and AT&T Locker.

None of these is essential to your phone operation, and can all be done at a later stage. However, doing them now will save you a little bit of time.

At this point, you will be redirected to your home screen.

Operational Basics

The Galaxy S5 is a very powerful smartphone with a host of supported apps and advanced features. However, it is important to first understand the basics of the interface and some critical features before getting into the more advanced capabilities of the S5. This section will help you understand the Galaxy S5's basic functions and interfaces.

To begin using your Galaxy S5, you will need to familiarize yourself with a few operational basics before you begin to learn the fundamentals of interacting with your phone.

Powering On/Off

It is not really necessary to ever turn your phone off, but you may want to do so from time to time, either to save battery life or simply to have time off from the phone. To turn your phone on, press and hold down the **power** button on the right side of the phone for a few seconds, until it begins to power on. After the device powers on and boots up, you should be taken to the lock screen, discussed below.

To power the phone down, hold the **power** button again for a few seconds. You will then see a "Device options" menu appear. From this menu, you can select "power off" which will shut down your phone. Once you select this option, you will see a message informing you that the device will shut down. Select "OK" from this popup dialog to continue the shutdown.

From this menu, you can also select "airplane mode" which will disable all radio communication to and from the device but still allow you to access content, apps and games which do not require a network connection. You may also choose to restart the phone. This is a useful function if you have been running your phone for several days and are noticing a lag or slowdown in normal operations.

Finally, you can select to "mute" your phone, change it to "vibrate" mode (meaning that it will still vibrate, but will not make any sound) or change it to "sound" mode, meaning that all regular sounds will occur during normal operation.

Charging the Phone

You can charge your Galaxy S5 at any time you desire. The phone can remain turned on, or be turned off while you are charging it. The Galaxy S5 will still be able to perform all normal functions while it is charging.

To charge your phone, take the USB cable, provided in your box, and plug the larger end into the charger head, also provided. The charger head is rectangular and black, with a typical two-prong electrical plug. Plug the charger head, with the USB cable attached into your wall outlet. Plug the other end of the USB cable, which should be thinner than the other end, with two distinct ridges, into the bottom of the Galaxy S5.

To reveal the S5's charger port, find the silver flap on the bottom of your phone with the USB symbol 🔌 etched into the plastic. With your finger, pry this cover away and pull the plastic flap to the side. You should see the charger point. Connect the available end of your USB charger to this port.

When you begin charging your Galaxy S5 it will make a quick sound, or, if it is on vibrate mode, vibrate quickly, to alert you that the charger has been connected. You will see a lightning bolt icon over the battery at the top of your phone's touch screen, and, at the lock screen, text will tell you that the phone is charging and provide the battery's percentage charge.

Power Saving Modes

Note that your battery will run down at very different rates, depending on how you use your phone. The S5's brilliant screen display alone drains a good amount of battery power, while running multiple, high-CPU intensive apps will also run down your phone's battery. Luckily, your Galaxy S5 comes equipped with two power saving modes, of varying degrees of severity, that help to automatically restrict battery use.

To view these modes, swipe down from the top of your screen to review your notification center, then tap the "settings" wheel, in the upper right hand corner, second icon from the right. In settings, swipe across the top categories to General, then tap it. Select "power saving" from the general menu.

Here, you will see two options: power saving mode, and ultra power saving mode. You can tap both to see descriptions of the functions that each performs, and to toggle these modes on and off. Power saving mode will modestly restrict CPU functioning and gives you the option to block background data, which may slow down or disrupt some apps' functions.

Ultra power saving mode, on the other hand, presents a radical reduction in battery usage, but will also alter your phone's appearance and abilities in many ways. In ultra power saving mode, your phone will convert to gray scale color, and you will only be able to use the most basic apps. However, your battery life will be greatly increased, allowing you to go many days without having to recharge your phone. While in ultra power saving mode, you will be shown how many days of power you have left remaining. To exit this mode, tap the options icon in the top right hand corner, then select "Disable ultra power saving mode." Your phone will return to its normal state.

You can also activate ultra power saving mode from your notification center. Swipe down from the top of the screen to open the notification center, then swipe left on the icons on top of the screen to reveal a second row of icons. You will see one icon of batteries with the text "U. power saving" beneath it. Tap this icon once to turn on ultra power saving mode.

Waking and Brightening the Phone

After a certain length of inactivity, your Galaxy S5's screen will dim, and then turn off entirely. To re-brighten a dimmed screen, simply swipe or tap your finger on the screen, and it will return to full brightness.

To awaken the phone after it has gone to sleep (meaning that its screen is completely dark) press either the **power** or **home** buttons, one time, quickly. You should return automatically to the lock screen. Please note that, when the screen dims, you will be able re-brighten to the same screen you were on when you last accessed the phone. If the phone has gone to sleep, you will need to unlock the phone again to access the previous screen.

Touch Screen Interface

The vast majority of your interaction with your Galaxy S5 will take place on its main touchscreen. The touchscreen is touch-sensitive, and, as you will quickly see, very accurate and responsive to even very small movements. You can perform most functions by tapping on the screen, swiping across or up and down, or by pinching and spreading your fingers. As you continue to use your Galaxy S5, you will become more accustomed to using these gestures to operate your phone.

Unlocking the Phone

The Galaxy S5 will automatically lock whenever it enters sleep mode. Sleep mode can either be brought on manually by the user, by pressing the **lock/power** button on the side of the phone, or come on automatically, after the phone has been idle for a specified amount of time. To set the length of idle time before the phone goes to sleep, see *Locking Your Home Screen,* below.

To wake up your Galaxy S5, press either the **lock/power** button, on the phone's right side, or the **home** button, located in the center at the bottom of your phone. Your screen should change from black to show your background image, along with the time, weather, and some other customizable features, if applicable.

You will notice that the phone is locked, meaning you cannot interact with it beyond reading the display

To unlock your phone, swipe across the touch screen, either from top to bottom or side to side. You will then be brought to the phone's home screen.

It is possible to require a passcode to unlock your screen, to add extra security to your phone's interface. To do so, please see **Locking Your Home Screen,** covered in the next section.

The Home Screen

Once you have unlocked your phone, you will land on the home screen page. The home screen contains some of your most commonly used apps and widgets. As with all Android phones, it is customizable to fit your desires.

Home Screen Basics

From your home screen, you can swipe left and right to access other screens. Other screens can be collections of apps or widgets. Swiping from the top of the screen to the bottom will reveal your notification center. For more information on the notification center, please see **The Notification Center**, below.

Also note your status bar, located at the very top of your touch screen. This bar provides valuable information. Generally speaking, you will be shown small icons representing data points about your phone status and usage. The status bar will show the time, your phone's battery life, signal strength, via network and Wi-Fi, and sound profile icons. It will also show if you have any pending notifications, or unread emails or texts, or missed phone calls. You can often find more information about symbols presented in the status bar by viewing the notification center.

As mentioned earlier, you can customize your home screen to feature the apps and widgets you prefer, but here is a quick explanation of some of the features that are present on the default home screen:

Weather Widget

On the top third of your screen, you will see a weather widget. In addition to telling you the weather in your area, this app gives you the time and date. Your Galaxy S5 will auto-detect your location and display the weather for your current location. You can tap once on the weather widget to see more information, including an extended forecast.

Google Search Widget

The Google search widget is the narrow bar in the middle of the screen. You can search Google from this widget by tapping once on this widget, and using the keyboard to input text into the search box on the next screen. This widget also allows you to use voice search. Begin by speaking "OK Google," aloud when the phone is open to its home screen. You can then speak your search terms aloud to perform a Google search, along with a host of other Google Voice capabilities.

Center Row Apps

Although these are set to certain apps by default, certain row apps are mutable and they do not appear on any other page, unlike the primary shortcut row apps.

Email – Input your personal email account information to use this app as your main email client.

Camera – Tap here to access your phone's camera.

Play Store – Tap here to access the Google Play Store, where you can download apps and games.

Google folder – Tap this folder to access all Google-specific apps, including Chrome web browser, Gmail, and Google Drive.

Navigation Dots

Navigation dots are small graphics between the center and bottom app rows. These show your position within launch pages. Individual pages are represented by square dots, with your Home screen's position shown by a small house icon. You will notice that these dots move to correspond to your movement through launch pages.

Primary Shortcut Apps

While also customizable, primary shortcut apps will appear on the bottom of each launch page. Therefore, it is a good idea to make these apps those that you use the most often, so that you can access them from any launch page. Your Galaxy S5 has selected the following commonly used apps, but you may change this if you like. You will receive more information about customizing these features in the coming pages.

Phone – Tap this app icon to enter the main phone screen, where you can place calls, check your call log, and access your voicemail, favorites, and contacts.

Contacts – Tap this app icon to access your contacts.

Messaging – Tap this app icon to enter the main text messaging window, where you can compose new text messages and view your received and sent texts.

Internet – Tap this app icon to access your Galaxy S5's native Internet browser.

Apps – Tap this icon to access your main apps menu.

The Notification Center

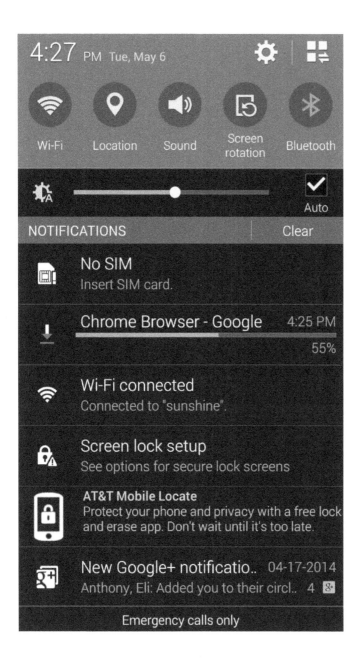

One of the most useful features on your Galaxy S5 is the notification center. This screen gives you information about recent emails or messages you've received, available software updates, and current weather and network settings. It is also a quick way to enable and disable critical S5 functions, such as Wi-Fi, Bluetooth, Sound, and Screen Rotation.

To access the notification center, swipe down from the top of any screen, including the lock screen. You will see the notification center when you scroll down from the top of your screen with your finger. Swipe down past the bottom of the touch screen, and the notification center will stay in place (see previous image).

On the top pane, you will see five icons: Wi-Fi, Location, Sound, Screen rotation, and Bluetooth. Tapping these icons is a quick way to enable or disable these features. A green-illuminated icon indicates that the feature is enabled, while a grey icon indicates that it is disabled.

Wi-Fi – Enabling the Wi-Fi feature allows you to see and quickly connect to local wireless networks. Your S5 will present you with available networks and show whether or not they are password protected. To join a network, simply tap the network name, and enter the password, if necessary.

Location – Enabling Location services helps your Galaxy S5 to determine your physical location in space. Many apps and services, such as weather and maps, depend on your Galaxy S5's location services being enabled to improve accuracy and provide data.

Sound – Enabling your sound will turn on your phone's sound profile, which may include interface sounds and ring tones. Disabling sound from the notification center window is a quick way to silence your phone. When the phone is in full sound mode, it will display a green-illuminated phone speaker icon. Tapping this icon once will change the phone to vibrate-only mode, and the icon will turn to a green-illuminated speaker with a slash through it and vibration symbols to its side. Tapping the icon once more will disable sound and vibrate entirely, and you will see a grey icon with a slash through it, indicating that the phone is in silent mode.

Screen rotation – Your Galaxy S5 is equipped with a screen that can display content in a vertically or horizontally oriented manner. While you will probably use the phone primarily in its vertical orientation, certain types of content, such as streaming videos, scale much better in horizontal landscape view. When you tilt your phone on its side, it will automatically reorient to horizontal landscape view, and rotate the screen view 90 degrees. If you wish to disable this feature, so that your phone will only display in vertical, portrait view at all times, tap this icon once, so that it is grey.

Note that certain content will also automatically display in landscape view, regardless of whether screen rotation is enabled or disabled.

Bluetooth – Bluetooth is a type of wireless network used to communicate over short distances, only between other Bluetooth enabled devices. These could include stereo systems or other smart phones. Enabling Bluetooth will turn on Bluetooth services and make your Galaxy S5 visible to other devices on the same Bluetooth network.

Managing Launch Pages

Once you've mastered the basics of the home page and the notification center, you will want to start managing your other launch pages. Launch pages can be designed and managed on a page-by-page basis, according to your specific desires. While the options are basically endless, there are a few overarching principles that are important to understand before you start building your pages.

Launch pages are easily accessed by swiping your finger left or right from the home screen or any other launch page. As you swipe between pages, you will notice that your location is marked by the **navigation dots** ¾ of the way down the page. You can return to your home page from any launch page by pressing the **home** button beneath your phone's touch screen. Note that you can also scroll between launch pages by tapping and holding on the **navigation dots** and then dragging across this row. You will see the launch page number appear on the bottom of your screen.

You can add or subtract launch pages as necessary, and are allowed a maximum of 7 pages, including your home screen. As we will see, this is more than enough room for all the widgets and apps you could want on your Galaxy S5.

Adding, Removing, and Moving Launch Pages

Your Galaxy S5 will automatically provide a few launch pages, preloaded with some of the S5's premiere apps and widgets. Remember that these are not set in stone – you can delete or move virtually anything that appears on the S5's pages at any time. However, you may choose to leave these in place for the time being, as you become accustomed to designing and using launch pages.

Adding a Launch Page

To add a launch page, make a "pinching" motion on an existing page, that is, place your thumb and index or middle finger apart on the touchscreen and move your fingers in towards each other, as if pinching the middle of the screen. You will see that the screen view zooms out to show the current page, as well as portions of pages to the left and right of the current page (see image).

You can also access this view by tapping and holding on a blank portion of any existing launch page, that is, an area where no apps or widgets exist. After holding your finger down for a moment, you should again return to the zoomed out view.

With the view still zoomed out, swipe your finger from right to left across the screen. You will scroll through all existing launch pages until you reach the end. The last available pane should be a blank launch page with a plus (+) symbol. Tap the plus symbol. You will see that the page has converted to a blank launch page. This is your newly created launch page.

Removing a Launch Page

To remove an existing launch page, the process is fairly similar. As before, pinch on the screen, or tap and hold on a blank spot on an existing page. You should again return to the zoomed out view, with your current launch page, and those to the right and left partially visible.

Scroll to the launch page that you would like to remove by swiping left or right across the screen. Once you have reached that page, tap and hold down on the page, while still in the zoomed out view. You will see a "remove" icon above the page, with an image of a trashcan. While still holding your finger on the touch screen, drag the launch page upwards, over the "remove" icon. Once you see the "remove" bar turn red, release your finger and the launch page will be removed from your phone.

Please note that, while you can add a new blank launch page, there is no way to recall recently removed launch pages, so make sure you are sure you want to delete the page before you remove it permanently.

Moving a Launch Page

It is easy to reorganize the position of existing launch pages so that your launch screens are arranged in an order that makes the most sense to you. Once you are familiar with adding and removing launch pages, it is easy to move existing launch pages around as well.

To do so, return to the zoomed-out page view, as before, by pinching or tapping and holding on a blank spot on any screen. Once you are in the zoomed-out view, tap and hold down on the page you wish to move. Without releasing your finger, drag the page to the right or left, in whichever direction you want to move it. Once you have reached the new desired position of the launch page, move your finger back to the center of the screen and release it. The page should drop into its new place.

Reassigning the Home Page

Your Galaxy S5 has pre-determined which launch page will serve as your home page, however, you can easily assign home page status to a different launch page if you so desire. To do so, return again to zoomed-out view by pinching on the screen or tapping and holding in a blank area of any launch page.

Once you are in the zoomed-out view, you will see that your current home page is outlined in white, and that the "house" symbol at the top of the page is illuminated.

To reassign your homepage, swipe left or right to the page you want to set as your new home page. Then, tap the "house" symbol at the top of the page. The page should now have a white outline and the "house" symbol should be illuminated white. Now, if you press the **home** button, you should be taken to your newly assigned home page.

Understanding Apps and Widgets

One of the ways in which the Android operation system that powers your Galaxy S5 differs from that of other smart phones is in the flexibility it offers the user. Nowhere is this flexibility more prominent than in the individual user's ability to create and manage launch pages to his or her liking.

Having said that, creating your own pages can sometimes present an overwhelming amount of choice. Before you begin assembling your own launch pages, it's important to first understand apps and widgets, the material that will eventually populate your launch pages.

Apps Versus Widgets

It is tempting to get hung up on mulling over the differences between apps and widgets, but there are not too many. Practically speaking, apps and widgets are essentially the same thing: programs that run on your Galaxy S5 (or any Android smartphone) and perform particular functions.

However, there is one very important difference between apps and widgets: apps are programs that show up as static icons on your launch pages. To begin interacting with an app, you must tap the icon to launch the program. Conversely, widgets are programs that are *already* running on your launch pages. They might update information in real time, change their display from time to time, or show you new data when prompted. You can often tap on widgets to launch other widget features, but you will see much of the program's activity happening right on your launch pages, without having to launch any program.

Once you understand this distinction, telling the difference between apps and widgets becomes very easy. Understanding this difference will help you when building your launch pages.

Managing Your Apps and Widgets

Now that you understand the difference between apps and widgets, you are ready to begin organizing, managing, and adding apps and widgets within your Galaxy S5.

Managing Apps

Generally speaking, you can access your apps in one of two ways: either by launching apps from a specific launch page, where you have placed their launch icon, or, by finding the app within the Apps folder. The Apps folder icon appears at the bottom, right-hand side of your touchscreen, in the primary shortcut row. As mentioned earlier, this primary shortcut row is permanently anchored to your phone touchscreen, so it will always appear, regardless of which launch page you are currently viewing. The Apps folder icon is the only launch icon which you cannot move to a different location.

The main difference between these two modes of access is one of ease. Presumably, apps which appear on your launch pages are those which you have already determined you will be using frequently enough that you would like them to be available on your launch pages. Conversely, the Apps folder will display *all* the apps currently installed on your phone. Therefore, it will require more searching to find the app you would like to access from within the Apps folder.

Note that you can scroll through the Apps folder much in the same way you navigate launch pages, by swiping from left to right or right to left across your screen. Apps are arranged alphabetically, so you can locate an app by finding its alphabetical place within this folder.

Regardless of whether you access your apps via your Apps folder or one of your launch or home screens, the same method applies for launching and moving apps.

Launching Apps

To launch an app, simply scroll to the app you would like to launch, and tap on it once. The app should then launch on its own. Some apps will require a few seconds of loading, while others will be usable immediately.

Moving Apps

Moving apps around your launch pages and on your primary shortcut bar is one of the easiest ways to quickly organize and personalize your Galaxy S5.

To move an app, first locate its current position on your phone. You may want to move an app from one launch page to another, or move an app from your Apps folder to a launch page. The process for moving an app is the same, regardless of its initial location. Once you have located the app, tap and hold on it. You will see the page "zoom out" and notice that you can move the app around by dragging it with your finger. You must keep pressing your finger on the screen for the duration of the app moving process. From this screen, you can reposition the app as you like:

To reposition the app on the same launch page: You will notice that, as you begin to drag the app icon around the page, empty squares will illuminate on the launch page to show available slots for the app. If you would like to drop the app within one of these slots, simply position the app over that square and then release your finger. If you would like to move an app icon to a position currently occupied by another app icon, move and drag it until it is hovering over the desired position. The app icon currently in its place will move to the next available place. You will then be presented with an empty illuminated square. Release your finger to drop the app into place.

To reposition the app on a different page: After you have tapped and held down on the app icon, you will notice a small diagram showing all existing launch pages at the bottom of the screen. Occupied space on each launch page is displayed as opaque boxes, while unoccupied space is transparent. While still holding on the app icon, drag the icon down to the diagram of the launch page you would like to place the app on. (see picture)

Hover the app icon over the launch page diagram, and you should be taken to the new launch page immediately. Once you are at this launch page, drag the app icon up into the new launch page. As when you relocate an app on the same page, you should again see empty squares that are illuminated on the border. To drop your app icon into any of these squares, simply drag the app over the square and release your finger. Your app should now be positioned on the new page.

To move an app from the Apps folder to a launch page: As discussed above, all of the apps stored on your Galaxy S5 will appear, in alphabetical order, in your Apps folder. You may want to move apps from your Apps folder to a launch page for easier access. Once you have located the app you wish to move within the Apps folder, tap and hold on it, as you would to move the app from within a launch page. You will a small diagram showing all existing launch pages at the bottom of the screen. Occupied space on each launch page is displayed as opaque boxes, while unoccupied space is transparent. While still holding on the app icon, drag the icon down to the diagram of the launch page you would like to place the app on. Hover the app icon over the launch page diagram, and you should be taken to the launch page within a few seconds. Once you are at this launch page, drag the app icon up into the new launch page. Drop your app icon into any of the illuminated squares, by dragging the app over the square and releasing your finger. Note that moving an app from the App folder to a launch page will not remove the app from your Apps folder. Your Galaxy S5 will simply make a copy of the app icon so that you will be able to launch your app either from the launch page or from your Apps folder.

Downloading New Apps

While many apps come preloaded on your Galaxy S5, there are many thousands more available for purchase or free download. There are apps for nearly everything, so it's definitely worth browsing available apps to enhance your experience with the S5. To find new apps, simply navigate to the Play Store app icon and tap on it. This will launch the Google Play Store, where you can discover new apps for your phone.

Managing Widgets

Unlike apps, widgets can only be accessed from launch pages. There is no central repository for widgets on the Galaxy S5. Your S5 will come preloaded with a number of widgets, some of which, such as the weather widget, have already been laid out on launch pages for you. However, many other widgets are preloaded on your phone, and accessible from the widgets menu.

Additionally, whenever you download a new app with widget capability, those widgets will also become available for us.

Moving and Resizing Widgets

Moving widgets which are already laid out on launch pages is easy, and very similar to the process of moving apps. To do so, first locate the widget you would like to move. Then, tap and hold on that widget. You will see your touchscreen transform to the zoomed-out view that you also use to move apps. To relocate your widget on the same page, simply drag it to the new desired position and then release your finger, dropping it into place. If another widget already exists there, it will move to the next available widget space to make room for the widget you are moving. If a row of apps exists where you would like to drop the widget, the whole app row will move to accommodate the new widget.

To move widgets from one launch page to another, tap and hold on the widget you'd like to move. Again, you will notice a small diagram of all existing launch pages near the bottom of your touch screen. Drag the widget down to hover over the image of the launch page where you would like to move your widget. Your view will then switch to this launch page. While still holding on the widget, drag it up into position and drop it in the new location.

It is important to note that, unlike apps, widgets have different shapes and dimensions, and so cannot be dropped in any location on your phone. Rather, they must be dropped into a space that is big enough to accommodate the widget size. While some widgets can be resized once they are dropped into place, your Galaxy S5 will not allow you to drop oversized widgets into a place where they will not fit. Therefore, it is important to first determine that you have enough space available to fit a widget where you would like to put it. If you don't have enough space, you must first move your existing apps and widgets to make room for the widget.

If it is possible to resize the widget, you can do so after you have dropped the widget into place. An orange bracket with four dots will appear around the widget, suggesting that you are able to resize the widget. Tap and hold on any one of the dots, and then drag to either expand or shrink the widget. Most widgets have resizing limits and will only allow you to expand or shrink them to a certain extent. Once the widget has reached its resize limits in either direction, the bracket will turn red and the widget will return to its previous size.

Introducing New Widgets

Adding new widgets to your launch pages is quick and easy. To see a scroll of your available widgets, navigate to a launch page with an empty space, that is, a part of the touchscreen that is unoccupied by apps or widgets. Tap and hold on the empty space, and within a few seconds, you will zoom out to the launch page edit view. Beneath the images of your launch pages, you will see three icons, "Wallpapers," "Widgets," and "Home Screen Settings." Tap on the "Widgets" icon.

You will then be taken to your main widgets menu. Here, you can peruse all available widgets. Note that the navigation dots at the bottom of your touch screen show how many pages of available widgets exist. As with your launch page navigation dots, you can tap and drag on the navigation dots to quickly skim through your widget pages. You can also swipe left or right on your touchscreen to navigate between widget pages (see widget menu picture)

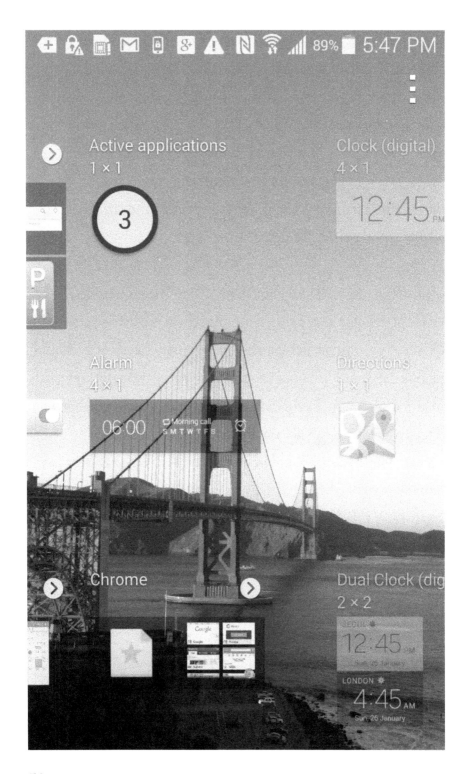

As you browse your widgets, you will notice that they are in different sizes and shapes.

Many widgets will have their dimensions written below their widget name, which makes it easier to ensure that you have created enough space for the widget on your launch page. A unit of 1 is equivalent to one square on a launch page, that is, the space which an app icon would ordinarily occupy. For example, if you would like to install a widget with 3x1 dimensions, you will have to clear a space of three horizontal squares and one vertical square. You will also note that some widgets have a small arrow icon, enclosed in a white circle, on the upper right side of the widget. This icon indicates that there are alternate display and size options available for that particular widget. To see these options, tap on the arrow icon. You will then be directed to a submenu showing the widget options.
Note that if the dimensions of a submenu widget differ from those of the main widget, these will be noted by the alternate widget.

Once you have settled on the widget you would like to install on your launch page, and cleared the appropriate amount of space for that widget, you are ready to move the widget from the widgets menu to the launch page. To do so, simply tap and hold on the widget. You will then be taken to the zoomed-out launch page view again. As before, note that you can navigate between launch pages on the diagram at the bottom of your touch screen. Select the launch page where you would like to position the widget by dragging and holding over that page image. Once you are transported to that page, drag and drop the widget into the appropriate place. At this point, you will have the opportunity to resize the widget, if applicable. Note that if there is insufficient space for the widget, you will not be allowed to drop the widget into place. You must clear up enough space, then attempt to drop the widget again.

Creating App Folders for Launch Pages

It may sometimes happen that you will want to create folders with specific apps housed inside the folders. You may want to do this to conserve space on your launch pages, or to create groups of similar apps that you can readily access from within a single folder.

To create a folder, first return to your apps menu, by tapping on the Apps icon on the primary shortcut row. Once you have accessed your apps main screen, click the menu icon in the upper right hand corner. This icon looks like three square dots stacked on top of each other. Select "create folder" from this pop-out menu (see screenshot).

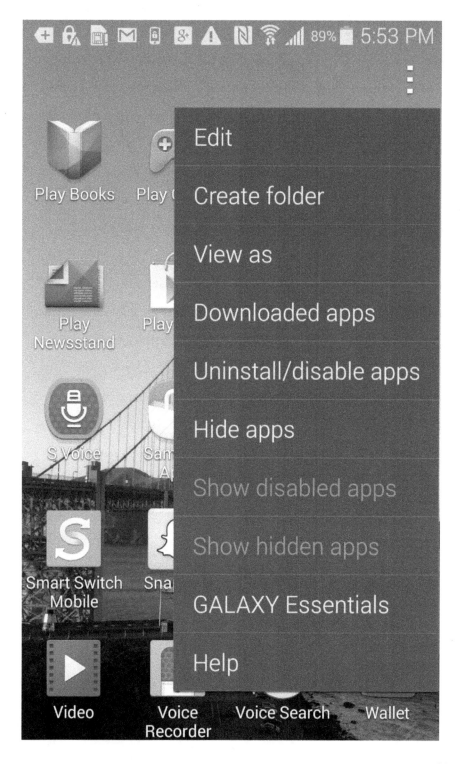

Edit

Create folder

View as

Downloaded apps

Uninstall/disable apps

Hide apps

Show disabled apps

Show hidden apps

GALAXY Essentials

Help

89% 5:53 PM

Play Books   Play

Play
Newsstand   Play

S Voice   Sam

Smart Switch   Sna
Mobile

Video   Voice   Voice Search   Wallet
Recorder

You will be prompted to enter a folder name from the popup dialog. You can name the folder after the category of app you plan to put in the folder, for example, "Social Media," or for the function of the apps in the folder, for example, "Navigation."

Once you enter the name of your folder, tap the plus sign below the text box. The popup dialog will disappear. Note that app icons now have an empty box to the upper left of the icon. To select the apps you would like to place in your newly created folder, tap on these empty boxes to check them off. When you have selected all the apps you would like to place in the folder, tap "done" in the upper right hand corner of your screen. You will now have a newly created folder in your Apps menu containing all the apps which you just placed in it. Note that when you place apps in a folder, they will *no longer* appear in your main Apps menu. Therefore, it is important to keep track of newly created folders and which apps they contain.

To move a folder to a launch page, follow the same process you would to move an ordinary app to a launch page. Simply tap and hold on the folder, drag it to the launch page you'd like to drop it on (from the zoomed-out launch page view), and drop the folder into place in its desired location by releasing your finger. (For a more in-depth explanation of placing apps and folders, please see **Moving Apps**, above.)

You can also create empty folders and add apps to them later, or add more apps to already existing folders. To do so, tap and hold on the app you would like to move into a folder. Drag the app to the folder's location, either on your launch pages or within the Apps folder, and hold it over the folder. After a second or two, the folder should become illuminated. Release your finger from the app and the app will drop into the folder. If you would like to remove an app from a folder, simply follow the process in reverse. Tap and hold on the app you'd like to remove, and then drag it outside of the folder view to reposition it on a launch page.

If you would prefer to move the app icon back to the Apps folder, meaning that it will not exist on any of your launch pages, tap and hold on the app, then drag it to the "Remove folder" icon on the top right side of your touch screen.

Managing the Primary Shortcuts Row
The last important point of managing your launch page displays consists in choosing the app icons which will occupy your primary shortcut row. Since this row is consistent across launch pages, it makes sense to choose the apps that you will use most

frequently, as you will want to have easy access to these from each launch page. Note that you are unable to move the Apps folder launch icon, and so you can only change the first four primary shortcut icons.

To change a primary shortcut, you must first have the app icon on an existing launch page. You cannot swap primary shortcuts directly for app icons that still reside in the Apps folder. Once you have located the app icon you would like to move to your primary shortcuts row, tap and hold on it, as with any other app you would like to move. Then, drag it down to the primary shortcut row, into the position you desire. The existing app should move to the new app's old spot on the launch page, while the new app will move to your primary shortcuts bar. You should now be able to access this app from any of your launch pages.

Launch Page Management

While organizing and laying out your apps is one of the most important parts of curating your launch pages, there are further changes you can make to your launch pages and home screen to enhance your phone's security and alter its visual appearance. These features range from essential phone safeguards to fun and creative ways to personalize your Galaxy S5.

Locking Your Home Screen

Locking your home screen is one of the most important security functions available on your Galaxy S5. By selecting a security method, you can ensure that no one will be able to access your phone's contents without your knowledge or permission.

To set a lock screen code, access your settings menu. To do so, swipe down from the top of the screen on any launch page, or on the lock screen, to reveal your notifications page. In the upper right hand corner, you should see a symbol of a "gear." Tap this symbol once to access your settings menu (see Settings menu screenshot).

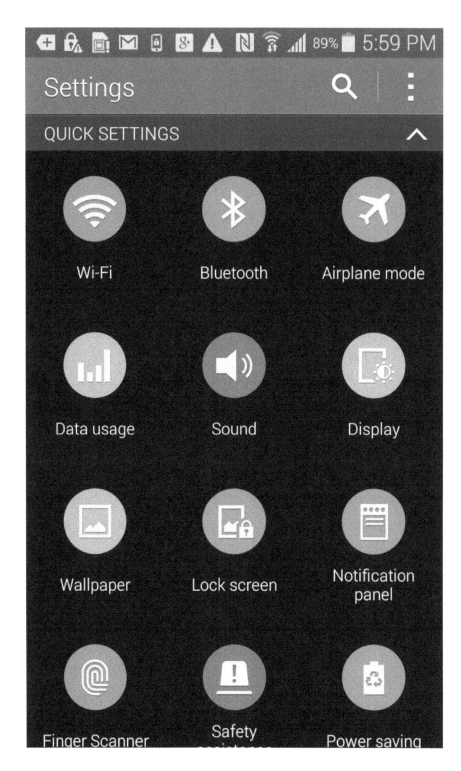

Once inside the settings menu, you can find lock screen settings both in the "Quick settings" and "Device" submenus. You can switch between submenus by tapping the text at the top of your touch screen. Pick either of the above mentioned submenu categories and swipe on the screen until you have found the "Lock screen" option. Tap this option to access the lock screen menu.

Within the lock screen menu, you will see various options pertaining to the lock screen. To set your security preferences, tap the top category, "Screen lock," under the "Screen security" text (see Lock Screen screenshot).

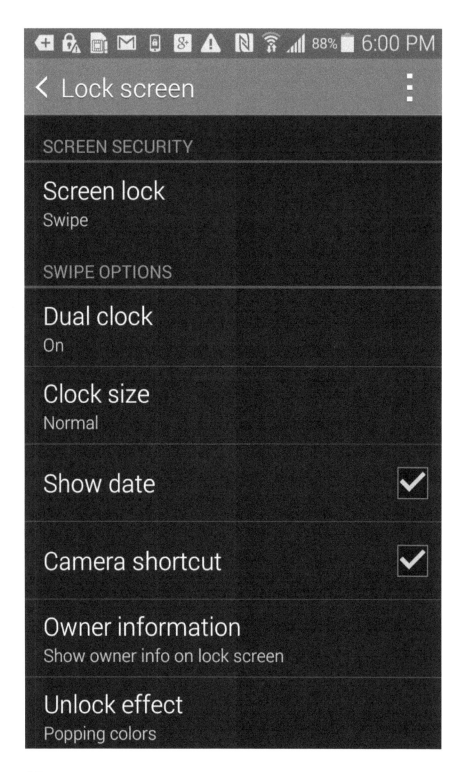

☐ 🔒 📷 M ▣ 8+ ⚠ N 📶 📶 88% 🔋 6:00 PM

‹ Lock screen ⋮

SCREEN SECURITY

Screen lock
Swipe

SWIPE OPTIONS

Dual clock
On

Clock size
Normal

Show date ☑

Camera shortcut ☑

Owner information
Show owner info on lock screen

Unlock effect
Popping colors

In this submenu you will see six different options, along with the level of security they provide for your phone. Explanations of each option appear below:

Swipe: The swipe option is the default setting for the lock screen. When you have this option selected, unlocking the screen merely requires you to swipe your finger across the screen before you will be taken to your home page. This is ranked as a no-security option, since anyone is capable of accessing your phone in this manner.

Pattern: In pattern unlock mode, you will be prompted to draw a pattern between nine dots to unlock your phone. This will be a pattern of your own devising, and it can be any pattern you can make between the nine dots. You will also be prompted to enter a PIN at this screen, in the case that you forget your pattern, although you will only be prompted to enter you pattern to unlock the screen. This is a medium security option because it requires special knowledge to unlock your phone, but is not impossible to guess.

Fingerprint: In fingerprint mode, your Galaxy S5 will take a scan on your fingerprint and save it, so that you can use it to unlock your phone. When you select fingerprint mode, you will be prompted to scan your fingerprint by sliding it against your S5's home screen button. Note that your S5 will have you scan the *same* finger eight times, and does not require a scan of all of your fingerprints. This is a medium to high security option.

PIN: In PIN mode, your phone will require a four-digit personal identification number before you can unlock it. You will be required to remember this number, so it is important to pick a four-digit number that is significant to you in some way, or easy to remember. This is a medium to high-security option.

Password: In password mode, you will be required to enter a longer password that can be comprised of letters, numbers, or symbols. This unlock mode is closer to the level of security required to access things like your email and social media accounts. This is a high-security option.

Once you have selected your lock method and entered the required information, you should also specify the amount of time you want your Galaxy S5 to wait before entering lock mode. This option will be found within the screen security menu, towards the bottom of the page. Swipe down until you reach "secured lock time." Tap this option once to select how long you would like your S5 to wait before entering locked mode. Note that locked mode differs from idle mode; when your phone is idle, it will shut off the screen to conserve battery and appear to "sleep," but you can still awake it quickly with the press of the power button, and will not be required to enter your lock information to access your phone's contents. However, when the phone has entered secure lock mode, you will need to enter your lock information before you are allowed to access the phone in anyway. The time span options for entering locked mode range anywhere from instantaneous lock to lock after one hour of inactive time. Choose the time length you prefer and tap it once to select it. You will see the black dot next to that option illuminate green to indicate that you have selected that choice.

Changing Your Launch Screen Wallpaper

Changing the wallpaper for your launch screens and lock screen is quick and easy and can add a personalized element to your Galaxy S5 display. You can change the wallpaper of your launch screens and lock screen individually, or set both to the same wallpaper. Your Galaxy S5 will come with a number of preloaded backgrounds, but you can also use an image from your personal photos as your wallpaper.

To change your background wallpaper, you must first navigate to your launch page settings. As before, you need only to tap and hold on an empty space on any launch page to access the settings page. Once you have arrived at this page, you will see three boxes with option text beneath them at the bottom of the touchscreen, "Wallpapers," "Widgets," and "Home screen settings." Tap "Wallpapers to access the wallpaper menu. The popup text will ask whether you want to set the wallpaper for the home screen, lock screen, or both the home and lock screen. For clarification, the lock screen is the first page you see when you wake your phone from sleep, where you are prompted to unlock your phone to access its contents. Conversely, changing the home screen wallpaper will change the wallpaper that appears on all launch pages.

Once you have decided whether to set the wallpaper for the lock screen, home screen, or both, you will be taken to the "Set wallpaper" screen. At the bottom of the screen, you can see the Galaxy S5's preloaded wallpapers. Swipe left to scroll through the wallpaper options. You will notice that, while some wallpapers are static images, others, such as the "Bubbles" and "Phase Beam" options are actually animations that will move around your screen. To select one of the Galaxy S5's preset options, scroll to that image and tap on it once. You will see that the new images fill your screen. To complete the action tap "Set wallpaper," which will appear either on the top of bottom of your touchscreen. Your new wallpaper should not appear on the screen for which it was selected.

If you would like to set one of your photos, instead of a Galaxy S5 preset, as the wallpaper image, tap on the box labeled "More images," that appears in the same row as the preset wallpapers. You will be taken to a roll of your camera photos. Choose the photo you would like to set as your wallpaper. You will then be given the image to crop the photo, if you would like. A blue bracket indicating the dimensions of the screen will appear along the edges of your photo. Tap and drag on the blue bracket to select the area of the photo you would like to use as your wallpaper. Once you have finished, tap "done" in the upper right hand corner of the touchscreen. Your Galaxy S5 will then set your photo as the new wallpaper.

Using Basic Communication Features

Now that you have acquainted yourself with the steps required to set up the appearance and organization of your Galaxy S5, you are ready to start using some of the basic and most essential features of the device. While many of these features will be familiar to users who have owned smartphones previously, it is important to acquaint yourself with the specifics of the Galaxy S5's operation of these features.

Managing Contacts

One of the most important parts of using any smartphone is managing and using your Contacts information so you can stay in touch with family, friends, coworkers, and your many other acquaintances. As with many smartphones, the Galaxy S5 can log the many different pieces of contact data within the same contact folder, making it easy to organize your contact information. Entering names and information into your contact folder also significantly expedites the calling, texting and email features available on the Galaxy S5.

Accessing, Communicating With, and Adding Contacts
To enter your contacts folder, simply locate the Contacts icon and tap it. Unless you have altered your primary shortcuts row, this is where you will find the Contacts icon. If you have moved

the Contacts icon from the primary shortcut row for any reason, you can find it in the Apps folder, accessed via the Apps icon on your primary shortcut row. (Since the Apps icon is permanently anchored to the primary shortcut row, this is often a good means of entry for tracking down apps you are having difficulty finding.)

Once you have accessed the contacts folder, you will see a list, organized alphabetically by first name, of your contacts. Note that if you have already synced your Google account, as you were prompted to do at your first phone startup, you will already have information on your Gmail contacts imported into your Contacts folder.

You can browse your contacts by swiping up and down within the main contacts window, or by tapping and dragging on the alphabetical scroll on the side. Tapping once on the side scroll is a good way of jumping quickly to a contact name. If you would like, you can also search for a contact name, by typing in the Search box near the top of your touchscreen, on the left side. Tap once in the box, next to the magnifying glass icon, and begin typing when the keyboard comes up. Many of the S5's text search functions are predictive, meaning that they narrow results progressively as you type, so make sure to watch the window below the search box to see when your desired contact pops up.

Communicating With Contacts

Tap a contact name once to be taken to that specific contact's page. There you will see all the contact information you have for that particular individual, which many include phone number(s), email address(es), or website(s). You can also see whether or not you are connected by any synced social media networks, such as Google Plus.

From this screen, you can communicate with your contact via any of the means displayed on the contact page. To call a contact, tap on his or her phone number. You will then be taken to the call screen and your phone call will begin. (For more information on phone calls, please see **Using the Phone**, below.)

If you would like to send an email to a contact, tap on his or her email address. You will be taken to your preferred email client app to begin composing your email.

If you have not yet logged a preference stating your preferred email client app, you will be prompted to do so at this stage. Your Galaxy S5 will display available email clients and ask you to select your preferred app. Once you have tapped on your choice, you will be asked if you would like to "always" use this app to send emails, or "just once." If you select always, you will not see this dialog anymore and will be directed straight to the app you choose at this stage. If you choose "just once" you will be prompted with this dialog every time you tap on an email link, whether within your Contacts folder, or elsewhere on your phone.)

To send a text message to a contact, tap the orange envelope icon at the top of the contact card, beneath the contact name and avatar. You will then be taken to Messages app, where you can begin composing your text message.

Adding New Contacts

Adding new contacts is a quick and easy process. To do so, tap the Contacts icon to launch your contacts app. On the top of the main Contacts screen you will see two rows; the first consists of four larger boxes (covered in the following pages) and the second row consists of a search box, followed by three icons.

To add a new contact, tap the Plus (+) sign, in the middle of the three icons. If you have a Google account synced with your device, you will then be prompted to determine whether you would like to sync the contact with your Google account, or only sync the contact with your Galaxy S5. Note that if you sync the contact with your Google account, you will still be able to access it from your S5; if you decide to only sync the contact with your device, you will only be able to access it from your S5, and will not be able to access it through other Google account means, for example, Gmail.

Once you have decided how you would like to sync your contact, you will be taken to the main contact information entry page. Here, you will be prompted to enter the name of the contact and all relevant contact information. To enter information in any of these fields, simply tap once inside that box. If there is no text box within a certain contact category (e.g., "Email"), tap the green plus sign to the right of that field, then tap inside the newly created text box. Once you do, your keyboard should pop up on the bottom half of the screen. It is wise to enter as much information as you have on an individual contact on this screen. There is no advantage to creating multiple contacts to house the same individual's phone, email, or other information, and, in fact, entering all of that information under the same contact name will streamline your Galaxy S5 use.

On this screen, you can also assign a profile picture to an individual contact, by tapping the plus (+) sign in the box that is currently occupied by an illustrated, generic contact picture, to the left of the "Name" field. You can choose to import a contact photo from your "Images," that is, photos that you have already taken with your Galaxy S5, from "Tagged Pictures," pictures on your Galaxy S5 or Google account that have already been tagged with individual's names, or, you can use the "Take picture" function, if you would like to snap a picture using your phone immediately to assign as a contact photo. Once you have set your contact photo, you will see this image when your contact calls your phone, or when you are searching in your Contacts folder.

You can also assign contacts individual ringtones. To do so, swipe down the individual contact information page, to "Ringtone," and tap it once. Here, you can pick among ringtones to assign one to that specific contact. All other contacts, unless also pre-assigned ringtones, will trigger your default ringtone when they call your Galaxy S5. Tap on your desired ringtone to set it as the default for that individual contact.

If you want to add another information field to the individual contact, tap "Add another field," at the bottom of the contact information screen. You will then be presented with a menu of other available choices. Tap the check boxes to the right of each field to add as many additional fields as you would like to that contact's page. Tap "OK" at the bottom of the page, and you will see that the new categories are now present on the contact information page.

When you have entered all your desired information, tap "Save" at the top of the page, and your new contact will be saved to the Contacts folder.

Editing, Favoriting, and Grouping Existing Contacts

Your Galaxy S5 offers many options to further expedite the process of finding and accessing contact information. You can also edit contact information at any time, so as to ensure that your contact list is always up to date and relevant.

Editing Contacts

To edit existing contact information, first locate the contact you want to edit. Once you find that contact's name, tap it to enter the main contact information page. You will see a large avatar with the contact's name on the top half of your touchscreen, along with the contact information, on the bottom half. On the top right side of the screen, you will see three icons: a star, a pencil, and three small rectangles in a stack, the option icon.

Unroll. me Support

Email / Home

support@unroll.me

Connected via

Groups

My contacts

To edit the contact information, such as the contact's phone number or email address, tap the pencil icon. You will then be taken to the contact edit screen. You can use the same steps discussed above, in "Adding New Contacts" to edit the contact's information, or to add more information. As before, tap "Save" when you are done editing and the contact's new information will be updated.

You can reveal further editing and management options by returning to the main contact information screen and pushing the "option" (or, "three rectangle") icon. You will see a dropdown menu with a number of additional options. The following is a short description of each of these options:

Delete – Delete the contact from your Galaxy S5, or from your Google account, if it is synced with your S5. Deleting the contact will delete all contact information as well.

Link contacts – Use this function if you have accidentally created two or more entries for the same contact, or would like to combine contact information from different entries into one contact. Tap the option, and then select the contacts you would like to link to that contact. Note that this contact will now serve as your master contact. Other contacts which you link to it will disappear from your normal contacts folder, and their information will be folded into this contact.

Unlink contacts – This action performs the reverse of "Link contacts." Unlink whichever contact you like by pressing the red minus (-) symbol to the right of the contact's name. That contact will unlink from the master contact and return to your general contacts folder, in its old position.

Mark as default – This option allows you to select which of your linked contacts you would like to mark as the default (master) contact. It also allows you to set one piece of contact information as the default means of contact for that individual, for example, defaulting to email or phone number.

Speed dial – You can set particular contacts to correspond to speed dial numbers which can be accessed via your phone keypad. (More on this in *Using Your Phone*, below). To assign a speed dial, tap this option from within the main contact information screen, and then choose the number you would like for your speed dial by tapping on it. If a contact name already occupies that speed dial spot, you will have the option to remove that contact speed dial by pressing the X to the right of the contact's name.

Share name card – If you would like to share your contact's complete information with someone else, this option allows you to do so. Contact information is shared via a .vcf file, a sort of digital business card. Most personal computers and smartphones are able to read .vcf files, so this can be a quick and convenient way to share contact information. The popup menu will display your options for sharing, including via text or email, or through other local network options such as Bluetooth or Wi-Fi, which allow you to share the .vcf file with other users on your shared network.

Send contact information – This option allows you to send the contact's primary information via text message.

Add to reject list – Select this option to add a contact to the reject list. Contacts on the reject list are indicated by a circle-slash icon next to their names in the main contact information page.

Remove from reject list – This option performs the reverse of the above action. Only available once you have added a contact to the reject list.

Add shortcut to home screen – Selecting this option will add a 1x1 icon for that contact to one of your launch pages. This option can be used for contacts whom you would like to be able to access directly from one of your launch pages. You can manage, move, and delete contact icons in the same way you do app icons.

Favoriting Contacts

As with many smartphone users, you will likely contact certain people more often than others. In order to facilitate this process, your Galaxy S5 provides a "Favorites" list that is readily accessible both from your main Phone and Contacts screens.

To favorite a contact, locate that contact's name in your main Contacts list, and go to that contact's record page. On the record page, you will see a "star" icon, in the top right corner of your touchscreen. Tap this star icon once to add a contact to your favorites list. (Tapping the star again will remove the contact.)

To access your favorites list, return to your main contacts page, where you can see the scroll of all existing contacts (typically accessible via your primary shortcuts row). On the top row, you will see the star icon with the text "Favorites," beneath it. Tap this icon to access your Favorites menu. You will see all of your favorited contacts, as well as a "frequently contacted" section, where individual with whom you have frequent contact are listed. To contact any of your favorites or frequent contacts, simply tap the icon with their name once.

Note that individuals on either of these lists will be contacted via the "default" means of contact, which you can set in the "mark as default" option, described above. Primary contact typically means default to phone number, but can also be set for other contact venues, for example, email address.

You can add new favorites to this screen by tapping the plus (+) sign in the upper right-hand side of the screen. You can also remove contacts from your favorite screen and change your favorites view mode by tapping the "option" ("three small rectangles") icon, next to the plus sign.

Grouping Contacts

You may want to organize your contacts into different groups. Groups can be useful in allowing you to contact multiple people with the same organization or for enabling quicker access to individual contacts.

To view your groups, tap the "Groups" icon, within your Contacts app, near the top of the page. It is located directly next to the search box and is a graphic of two people. If you have synced your phone with your Google account and have groups specified on your Google account (for example, work-related email groups) these may already appear here. Otherwise, your Galaxy S5 will suggest a few groups you may want to populate with contacts, such as friends, family, etc.

To add a new group, tap the plus (+) sign at the top of the touchscreen. You will then be taken to the group creation screen, where you can name the group, set a default ringtone, and, of course, add members. Once you have set your group preferences, tap "Save" and your new group will now appear in your Groups list.

To add a new contact to an existing group, scroll to that group within this window, and tap on it. You can either tap the plus (+) sign at the top of the group's page, or just begin searching for the name of the contact you would like to add in the contact box. Tap the check box next to that contact's name, and then press "Done" in the upper right hand corner. You can add as many contacts to the group as you want using this method. These contacts will now be part of your group.

To delete an entire group, go to the main Groups window and tap the "option" tab, in the upper right hand corner, next to the plus sign. Here, you will see options to delete groups or change the group order. If you select "change order" you will be able to drag different group names around into the list order in which you would like to see them presented. If you pick "delete group" you will be prompted to select the group you would like to delete. Note that you cannot delete groups that are preloaded on the S5, only those that you have created yourself.

Messaging Groups

To message all group members simultaneously, locate the group you would like to message it in the main Groups screen. Once you have opened this Group window, tap on the "option" button, in the upper right-hand corner, next to the plus sign. Here you will see options to remove an individual contact from the group, edit group settings, or to send a message or email.

To message all members in the group, tap on this last option "Send message or email." You will be prompted to select which you would like to send from the popup dialog, and then asked to pick which members of the group you would like to contact, or to select all group members by tapping the check boxes. You will then be directed to the appropriate app, either your email or texting app. Note that you can also group text from within the text app, explained in *Messaging*, below.

Using the Phone

With all the features available on your Galaxy S5, it could be easy to forget that the S5 is, at its most essential, a portable phone. And, odds are, that you will be using your Galaxy S5 as way to place and receive phone calls quite often. Given this, it is important to understand some of the basic features of making, receiving, and managing phone calls. If you have already set up your contacts list, as outlined above, many of these processes will be made much easier.

The phone app icon is, as a default, located leftmost on your primary shortcut row. It is recommended that you keep either your Phone or Contacts launch icon in the primary shortcut row, as you will depend heavily on readily accessing your phone and contacts during normal phone operation.

Tap the phone icon once to be taken to the main Phone page. It is important to note at this stage that the Phone and Contacts pages are *linked*. That is, you are presented with the same options on your Phone page as on your Contacts page. Action which is undertaken on either page will be reflected on the other one. It is for this reason that we recommend keeping *one* of the two in your primary shortcut row, while it is unnecessary to keep both. Generally speaking, your Contacts launch icon will usually bring you to the main contacts screen, while the Phone launch icon will bring you the keypad screen. However, these are contained within the same app, and are easily accessed within that app.

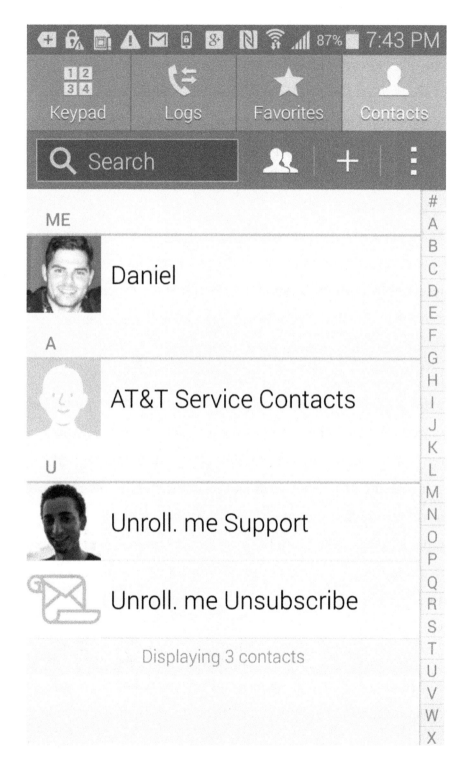

Since the **Favorites** and **Contacts** pages have already been covered above, this section will focus on the **Keypad** and **Logs** functionality. You will see that these are the four main page screens available, at the top of the main Phone/Contacts page.

Using the Keypad

The Galaxy S5 keypad operates like a normal touch-tone phone, but with added functionality. On the main keypad screen, (accessed by tapping "keypad" on the top of the touch screen from within the Phone/Contacts app), you will see a number grid, along with some other button options.

To dial a phone number, simply begin tapping out the number on the keypad. You will notice that the number begins to fill the grey box above the keypad. Note too that your Galaxy S5 will again activate its predictive functions in the slender blue box above the number window. You will see that, as you type the number, your S5 will attempt to predict the phone number you are attempting to call. You can select one of your preexisting contacts from this predictive box at any time by tapping on that field.

If the phone number you enter is not recognized by the S5 as belonging to one of your preexisting contacts, the predictive box will instead display the text "+ Add to Contacts." If you would like to add this number to your contacts list, tap this text. You will then be taken to an "Add to Contact" popout. From this screen, you can either create a new contact, or update an existing contact, meaning that will add the phone number to a contact name already in your address book. Tap the corresponding option to either update or add a new contact.

If you make a mistake while inputting a telephone number, simply use the "delete" icon at the bottom right side of the keypad. It looks like a leftwards-facing arrow with an X in the center. The delete button will delete one character at a time, from right to left.

Once you have input your desired telephone number into the keypad screen, you can begin your call by pressing the green telephone icon in the middle of the keypad, at the bottom of the touchscreen. This will start your call.

You can also start a call by pressing and holding on one of your preset speed dial numbers. For example, if you would like to call the contact whose speed dial is set to the number "4," tap and hold on the "4" button for a moment. You can also access your speed dials by tapping the speed dial number once and then pressing the green call button. This is especially useful for contacts with two digit speed dials.

Beyond call functions, you can also access your voicemail from the keypad screen, by tapping the voicemail icon, a cassette tape in the lower left corner of the keypad. You can also toggle sound, vibrate, and silent mode by tapping and holding on the pound (#) key.

Using Logs

You can also interact with your contacts via the Logs screen. To access the Logs screen, tap the tab next to "Keypad," within your Phone/Contacts screen. You will be taken to the logs screen which keeps a running record of your recent incoming and outgoing calls and texts. An individual call or text log will display the name of the contact, if known, or the phone number, if the contact is unknown to your Galaxy S5. It will also display the time of the call or text, whether the communication was sent or received by you, and whether or not the call or text has been answered. The arrow symbols beneath each log contact name will tell you this information:
- An arrow facing right that is red in color indicates that communication is outgoing, meaning that it was sent by you to another recipient.

- An arrow facing left that is green in color indicates that communication is incoming, meaning that it was sent by someone else, to you.

- A blue circle with a slash through it means that your call was rejected by the person you were trying to reach. This could be because of an auto-reject feature, indicated by an "A" next to the circle and slash, or because the person you were trying to reach manually rejected your call.

- Both incoming and outgoing calls are indicated by a telephone icon, next to a red or green arrow, which, as mentioned above, indicate whether the call was outgoing or incoming.

- Incoming and outgoing text messages are indicated by an envelope icon, next to, as with phone calls, a green or red arrow indicating whether the text was incoming or outgoing.

- Media messages are shown as envelops, but with a "movie reel" icon in the lower left side of the envelope. These are also shown as incoming or outgoing.

- An incoming missed call is indicated by a red phone next to the usual phone icon with a grey arrow bouncing off that phone. Receiving a missed call means that your phone notified you of the incoming call, but that you did not answer it.

To quickly respond to any contact who appears in your Logs, you can swipe on the contact's name. Swiping across the contact's name from left to right will place a call to that contact. Swiping in the other direction, from right to left, will allow you to compose a text message to that contact. You can also interact with a contact by tapping once on their log, and then selecting the call or text tabs from beneath the contact name. You can also choose to view the contact profile from this screen.

You can also search your Logs menu, by tapping in the box in the upper left hand corner of the touch screen, with text that reads "All calls." Tap in the box and type your search terms to look for a call.

The "options" key, to the right of the search box, will also provide you the ability to perform more functions within your Logs menu. Among the most useful are the "delete" function, which will allow you to delete any logs of calls or texts you have received. To delete a log, tap the delete button, from the options menu. You will then be prompted to mark check boxes for the items that you wish to delete from your log. You can also "select all" if you would like. Tap the check boxes of the items to delete, and then press the delete key again. Your log will be cleared of those items.

In-Call Features

Once you have begun a call, there are a number of phone options which can still be executed whilst your call is underway. To see these options, merely tilt the phone away from your ear, so that you are looking straight at it without moving your head. If you are using a headset, you may need to press the power/wake button on the side of the phone to see these options.

There are six major in-call functions, with some variance depending on the type of call you are conducting. Understanding these options is important to correct in-call operation of your Galaxy S5:

Add call: You can use this setting, while in one call, to add another call, in order to create a conference call.

Keypad: Tap this button to reveal your phone's keypad, while in the middle of a call. This may sometimes be necessary, such as when you are required to input number selections at automated phone prompts.

End call: Tap this button to end your call. If the person on the other end hangs up first, your call will end automatically.

Speaker: Tap the speaker icon to active the phone's speakerphone. When speakerphone is activated, you will no longer need to hold the phone to your ear or use a headset.

Mute: Tap the mute key to disable audio on *your end* of the call. You will still be able to hear the person on the other end of the phone call, but he or she will not be able to hear you when you speak. Tap the icon again to unmute your phone and proceed with your conversation.

Bluetooth: Tap this icon to activate your Bluetooth enabled headset. You will then be able to speak into your headset to conduct your phone call. Note that this is only necessary when using a Bluetooth headset; a wired headset equipped with a microphone will be automatically detected by your phone.

Receiving Incoming Calls

When someone calls you, you will be notified by your desired method (i.e., ring tone, vibrate, personalized ring tone, silent display only). Your touch screen will display the contact's name, if known, and the telephone number, in either case. Your phone will also display the caller's avatar photo, if you have set one in your Contacts page. To answer/accept the call, tap on the green phone icon and drag from left to right. To reject/ignore the call, tap on the red phone icon and drag from right to left. If you would prefer to ignore the call and send a text message instead, drag up from the bottom of the screen. Here, you will see some of your preset response text messages, explained in **Other Texting Features**.

You can also take no action, in which case the phone will ring a few more times, then direct the caller to your voicemail.

Using Conference Call

You can use your Galaxy S5 to facilitate a conference call between multiple callers. To do so, call a contact as you would normally. Once that contact has answered and you have established a connection with him or her, tap the "Add Call" option from your in-call options. You will then be redirected to your contacts menu, where you can add another caller. You will now see both contact names and the duration of the respective calls displayed on your touch screen. Once you establish contact with the second contact, you will notice that the "Add Call" option has been replaced by a "Merge" option. Tap this to merge the calls into one conference call. You can tap "Add Call" again to add another user to the conference call, and so on.

Note that not all of your contacts will have mobile phones that are able to join a conference call hosted by your Galaxy S5. It is also important to remember that, since you are the host of the conference call, once you disconnect, all other participants will also be disconnected. However, if an individual participant other than you hangs up, the conference call will continue normally.

Messaging

One of the most important features of your Galaxy S5 is its messaging function. Increasingly, text messaging is becoming one of the dominant means of informal communication for mobile phone users. While many users who have had experience with smartphones in the past will be familiar with the basic methods of smartphone texting, the S5 has some important texting features that set it apart from other smartphones on the market.

Messaging Basics

As with your phone, contacts, and Internet, the developers of the Galaxy S5 thought your Messaging app critical enough to include it as a default on your primary shortcut row. Although messages can be sent from other apps, such as via your Contacts app, we recommend leaving the Messaging launch icon in its place on the primary shortcut row, as this is your most direct route to accessing, reading, and responding to text messages.

Tap the Messaging icon to be taken to the main messages screen, where you will see a log of your incoming and outgoing text messages. Unlike with your phone call log, text messages do not specifically indicate whether they are incoming or outgoing in your text log. In your text log, you will see the name of the person with whom you are texting, and some preview text below the contact name, showing the first sentence or so of the text. You will also see the contact avatar to the left of the contact name and text preview.

Composing and Responding to Texts

To compose a new text, tap on the pencil icon in the upper right hand corner of the touchscreen, between the search and options icons. You will then be taken to the new message screen. To find the contact you would like to message, begin typing in the "Enter recipients" box. The cursor should default to this location. Note, again, that the S5 will attempt to predict your intended recipient as you type, so keep an eye on the window below the search box. Once you have entered once recipient name, you can keep add recipients, if you would like to send a group text. Alternatively, you can tap the "man" icon to the right of the "Enter recipients" box to select one of your already-created groups to text.

When you have finished entering recipient names, tap the box in the window below that reads "Enter message." You can now begin composing your text message.

Using the Keyboard

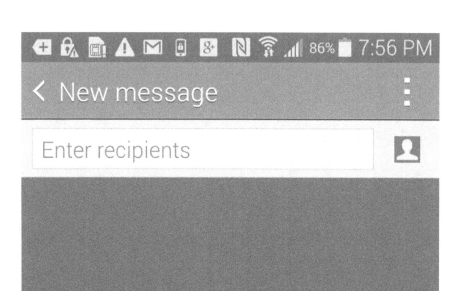

New message

Enter recipients

Enter message

160/1

The | I | You | >

1 2 3 4 5 6 7 8 9 0

Q W E R T Y U I O P

A S D F G H J K L

Z X C V B N M

English(US)

While you will use your Galaxy S5 keyboard to perform many different functions on your smartphone, it's import to familiarize yourself with some basic points on its operation, especially as it pertains to keyboard-heavy activities, such as texting. Many of the techniques described below are utilizable in all text intensive formats, including email and Internet use.

Your keyboard is laid out in QWERTY format, just as your computer keyboard, so it should look fairly familiar to you. Your S5 will default to a capital letter at the beginning of every sentence. It will also usually autocorrect for proper nouns, so that you do not have to manually input a capital letter. If, at any time, you wish to manually add a capital letter, simply press the "up arrow" icon, located next to "Z" on the keyboard, and it will toggle the keyboard to display capital letters only. Pressing this arrow again will toggle the keyboard back to lowercase mode. On the opposite side of the touch screen, you will see the delete key, a leftwards-facing arrow with an X on it. Tap this key once to backspace one character at a time. If you tap and hold on this key, the S5 will continually delete text until you release the key, at a progressively faster rate. This is a good way to quickly delete all the text in the message you are composing, if you would like to start over. Beneath the delete key is the hard return key, an arrow pointing left with a right angle bend in it. You can use this to jump down a line in your text, inserting a hard return. Remember, too, that tapping the space bar twice quickly, to indicate the end of a sentence, will automatically insert a period and reset the keyboard to capital letters.

On the opposite side of the phone, beneath the "up arrow" is the "Sym" or symbol key. Tapping this once will show the menu of available preset symbols. You can insert any of these symbols as you typically would a letter, by tapping on them. Notice that the "Sym" key has changed into a key reading "ABC." Tapping this once will return you to your letter keyboard. Notice too that above the "ABC" key is a "1/2" key, indicating that you are on page 1 of 2 available pages of symbols. Tap this key again to go to page 2.

You can also access certain oft-used symbols from your ABC keyboard. If you look closely at the letters on your keyboard, you will notice that each has a smaller symbol in the upper right-hand corner. If you tap and hold on one of these letters for a moment, a popup window will give you the option to select that symbol. Note that you can also use this method to insert letters with accents or special characters.

As you type, your Galaxy S5 will again use its predictive function to guess the word you are spelling. If, at any point, you see the word you would like to use in the black box beneath the text window, simply tap on it and it will be inserted into your message. You can also tap the white, right-facing arrow on the side of your text suggestions to see an expanded list of suggestions.

To edit your message, tap once on any part of the message. You will see the cursor jump to that spot, and the blue editing arrow will appear. Tap and drag on the arrow to move the cursor to the spot you would like to edit. Once there, you can delete or insert text.

You can also select parts of text to edit or copy. To do so, tap and hold on the word you would like to select. After a moment, you will see the word highlighted in blue, with a blue cursor on either side of it. You will also see popup text with four options: select all, cut, copy, and dictionary. Tapping "select all" will highlight all the text in the body of the message. Tapping "cut" will remove this part of the message, but save the text so that you can insert it elsewhere in the message, using the paste function. Tapping "copy" will copy that part of the message, but leave the text in place. Tapping "dictionary" will open the dictionary app so you can look up the word's definition. To highlight a particular part of a phrase, you can also drag the blue cursors beneath the highlighted word. Dragging the right cursor will highlight text to the right of the word, while dragging the left cursor will highlight text to the left. Make your selection using these cursors and then tap "cut" or "copy."

To paste text you have cut or copied, tap and hold on an empty space within the text entry window. You will see the blue cursor return, and see the options "Paste" and "Clipboard." To paste the most recent word or phrase you cut or copied in that location, tap "paste." If you would like to select from among words and phrases you have recently cut or copied, tap "clipboard." A window revealing your recently copied text will appear. Tap your choice from among your clipboard options and it will be inserted into the text box.

If you would like to attach some type of media to your text message, tap the paperclip icon immediately to the left of the text window. You will then be given a list of media and data points you can send via text. These include standard media, such as video, audio, and photos. You can also send audio recordings of your voice (using "Record audio"), memos, calendar events, and contacts, or send data on a physical location ("My location" or "Maps").

You can also insert emoticons, small pictographs, into your text messages. To do so, tap on the smiley face icon to the left of your text window. You can drag up and down to see the available emoticons within a particular menu. Or, tap on the icons on the orange bar between the text and emoticon windows to access different menus of emoticons, grouped roughly by theme. Tap once on any emoticon to insert it into your text message.

Once you have finished composing your message, tap the orange envelope icon on the right of the text window to send it. You will see your message appear in the message window above the text window. Texts sent by you appear on the right side of the window, while texts sent by others will appear on the left side of this window.

If, at any time, you would like to delete any or all of the text messages in a particular conversation, simply tap the trash bin icon on the top of the touchscreen. Select which messages you'd like to delete (or tap "select all"), and then tap "delete" on the upper right-hand side of the touchscreen.

Other Texting Features

Beyond the usual texting functions, your S5 also provides you with many other ways to enhance your texting experience. Here are some other useful texting functions:

Quick responses – You can create text templates for messages that you send frequently or for particular situations. Your Galaxy S5 comes preloaded with a number of common responses, but you can also set your own. To access quick responses, tap the pencil icon to compose a new text, and then tap the "option" key, in the upper right hand corner of your touchscreen. Tap in the text composition window, so that you see the cursor flashing. Then, tap "quick responses." Here, you will see a list of preset quick responses, as well as any that you have created as a user. Tap one of these options to have it inserted into the body of your text message.

To create your own quick response, access the main messaging window, where you can see all of your text conversations. Tap the options icon in this window, next to the pencil icon, and then tap "Settings." From the Settings menu, tap "quick responses." Then, tap the plus (+) icon in the upper right hand corner. Type the text of the quick response you would like to create in the text box (up to 200 characters), and then tap "Save." Your quick response will now be available. You can also delete unwanted quick responses (including the S5's default quick responses), by tapping the trash can icon above the plus sign and selecting those which you would like to delete.

Scheduled messages – Using this feature, you can compose texts ahead of time, and then have your Galaxy S5 send these messages at a particular time to your chosen recipient. To do so, first compose and address a text message as you normally would. Then, still within the text composition screen, tap the options icon in the upper right hand corner. Select "Schedule message" from the dropdown menu. You will then be prompted to pick a date and time when you would like the message to be sent. Select your desired send time, then tap "done."

Voice dictation – You can also dictate text messages to your phone via your spoken voice. To do so, begin composing a text message as you normally would, by tapping the pencil icon within the Messaging window. Tap in the message window to bring up the keyboard. Between the "Sym" and comma keys, you will see a key with a small microphone icon. This is your voice texting key. This icon is not always present on your keyboard, but whenever you see it, it means that voice dictation is enabled.

Tap on the icon once to begin voice dictation. You will see a microphone icon in the lower half of your screen, illuminated red. As you start speaking, you will notice that the circle around the microphone illuminates red, indicating that your Galaxy S5 is picking up your voice. When you are done dictating, tap the microphone icon again. You will see the dictated text appear in your text window above. If you would like to continue dictating, tap the microphone icon again and speak again. The new text will be inserted after the existing text.

To return to the keyboard and stop voice dictation, tap the keyboard icon to the left of the microphone icon.

Using Email

Your Galaxy S5 comes with a built in email client of its own, aptly called "Email." This is a native email app that is separate from client-specific apps, such as Gmail (although a Gmail app also comes preloaded on your S5). While not absolutely necessary, using the S5's native app is often faster than using any third party app, and integrates more thoroughly with your S5.

Setting Up Your Email

When you first open your email app, you will be prompted to enter your email data. Here, you can enter the username and password you typically use to sign into your email account, regardless of what email client you use. Remember that you must add your full email address, since your Galaxy S5 will not intuitively know what client you use. That means you must type "john.smith@yahoo.com" not merely "john.smith." Enter your email data, then hit "next."

You will know be prompted to set a few account preferences. You can choose the period for which you would like to sync the email, that is, how far back in time you would like your S5 to retrieve emails from your inbox. You can also set your sync and peak schedules, which tell your phone how often to query the server for new emails. Your sync schedule is how often your S5 will normally check your email, while your peak schedule is how often your S5 will check for email during "peak hours," times of heightened activity which you can specify. Note that the more frequently you have your S5 check for new emails, the faster your battery life will go down.

After you have set your preferences on this screen, you will be prompted to give the email account a name if you like (for example, your name, e.g. "John Smith," spelled correctly). This is the name that will be displayed on outgoing images, so it's important that it at least somewhat resembles your given name.

Note that you can add more than one email account to your Email app, so that you can have all of the email from your different email accounts housed in the same app.

To do so, tap the options key in the upper right hand corner of your Inbox screen. Tap "settings" at the dropdown menu, and then tap "Manage accounts," at the next menu screen. You will see a plus (+) sign on the top bar, next to the options icon. Tap the plus sign, and you will be taken back to the now-familiar email configuration screen. Enter the details for this new account just as you did for your first email account. You can follow the same steps to add further accounts.

Once you have added multiple accounts, your inbox will default to "combined inbox," meaning that you will see all the email from all your email accounts. However, it is easy to toggle between accounts. To do so, tap the three bar icon, at the top left of your touch screen, just to the left of the text "Combined inbox." A window will pop out showing each of your added accounts. To move between these accounts, simply tap on the blue bar with the account name you'd like to access. Then, when the account information expands, tap "Inbox." Your inbox will now show emails for that account only. You can follow these steps to access your other added accounts, or to return to the combined inbox.

You can also access other relevant email folders in this manner, including your email drafts, and your sent email outbox, as well as any other folders you have created within your email account.

Using Email Features

Composing an Email

To begin composing an email, tap the pencil icon in the lower left corner of your touchscreen. You will then be redirected to the composition window on your touchscreen. Enter your recipient's email address in the "To" box, using the keyboard, and keeping an eye out for the S5's predictions. If you see the name of your recipient pop up in the prediction window below, simply tap that person's name to insert his or her email address. You can also address an email to a group by pressing the "man" icon to the direct right of the "To" box. Tap the down arrow to the right of this icon to reveal boxes where you can Cc (carbon copy) and Bcc (blind carbon copy) additional recipients.

When you have finished addressing your email, tap in the subject box, and fill it out, if you desire. You can then tap the "Next" key, in the lower right hand corner of your keyboard to begin typing in the body of your email.

When you have finished typing your email, you can send it by tapping the icon of the piece of mail with a right-pointing arrow in the upper right-hand corner of the touchscreen. You will then be returned to your main email inbox. If you'd prefer to save a draft of the email so you can return to it later, tap the floppy disk icon, second from the left, in the top row. The email will then be saved in your drafts folder. If you would like to discard the email, tap the "X" icon, third from left on the top row.

Additional Email Features

Your S5's mobile email possesses many of the same features as your web or program based email on your personal computer. Some of these capabilities are described below.

In your inbox window, you can press the circular arrow icon, second from the left on the bottom, to refresh your inbox at any time. This will manually query the server for new emails. Tap the magnifying glass icon next to it to search your inbox for emails by names or subjects. Tap the file icon to see the different folders available within your inbox.

A special feature of your Galaxy S5's native email client is its ability to delay sending your email for a few seconds after you tap the "send" icon. This can be useful if you accidentally send the email before you mean to, or if you change your mind about sending it. To manage this feature, tap the options icon from the main inbox screen, then tap "Delay email sending." Tap the check to ensure that delay email sending is on, and then specify the length of time you'd like your S5 to wait before sending the email. Now, right after you send an email, you will see text at the bottom of your S5's screen allowing you to stop the email from sending. After the length of time you specified, this text will disappear and your email will go out.

There are also some important features to understand that are available from within your email composition window:

Attach documents – To attach a document, tap the paperclip icon, leftmost on the upper row. You can attach images, saved files, audio, and contact information, such as contacts or address data.

Undo and redo – Tap the curved left-facing arrow directly above the text box to undo your most recent typing. Tapping the curved right-facing arrow next to it will redo your typing.

Insert picture – Tap the landscape icon above the text box (to the right of the redo arrow) to insert an image from your phone into the body of the email.

Font size – Tap the "11 px" icon, to the right of the landscape icon, to change your text size. You can select any text size from the available range at the popout dialog.

Bold and italics – Toggle bold and italic font by pressing the "**B**" or "*I*" icons directly above the text box.

As with text messages, you can also schedule your email to be sent out at a specific time. To do so, tap the options icon within the email composition window. You will see an option to "schedule email." Tap this option and then set the time and date when you would like the S5 to send your email.

Using the Internet

Your Galaxy S5's native browser is designed for ease of use that makes abundant use of the S5's beautiful screen resolution. While there are many myriad options for Internet use, this section covers the basics of navigating the Internet using the S5's native browser.

Launch the Internet app by tapping the "Internet" app icon, anchored by default to the primary shortcut row. You will be launched to the S5's default homepage, and can begin surfing the Internet immediately. It's recommended that you are connected to Wi-Fi while surfing the Internet, but your network connection will also do.

 Web   Images   Sign in

Thank you to all the teachers on Earth.

The Internet navigation toolbar is located at the top of your touchscreen. You can type in any URL (Internet website address) you want by simply tapping in the box and using the keyboard to type. Tapping the Globe icon to the left of the URL bar will allow you to select navigation to one of several popular search sites.

To the right of the URL bar, you will see a "windows" icon with a number. This displays the number of web windows currently open. To see all open windows, tap this icon once. You will be presented with all your open windows, on the right side of your screen. You can swipe between windows, and then tap on the one you would like to view.

Tapping the options icon to the right of the URL toolbar will provide you with some of the Internet browser options. Some useful options are:

Homepage – Sets the current page as your browser's new default homepage.

New window – Opens a new browser window, similar to opening a new tab in your PC's Internet browser.

Add to quick access – Adds a frequently visited website to your quick access page. You can view your quick access page by tapping "new window" then selecting "Quick access" from the available windows on the right side of your screen.

Add shortcut to home screen – Adds a launch icon to one of your launch pages from which you can immediately access the website.

Save page – Saves the data on the page for offline or later perusal.

Share via – Allows you to pick a social media or communication app through which you can share that particular web page.

The bottom row of your Internet browser features basic navigation features like the back, forward and home buttons. There is also a saved page icon, where you can view your saved pages, and a bookmarks icon, where you can manage your bookmarks.

Tapping the bookmarks icon once will allow you to view your existing bookmarks. Tapping the plus (+) sign in the top right hand corner will allow you to save the current page to your bookmarks window.

Using Your Camera and Accessing Media

Among the best features of your Galaxy S5 is its powerful camera. With its 13-megapixel resolution, zoom functions, and picture taking modes, the S5 possesses one of the most powerful and versatile cameras available in a smartphone. Familiarizing yourself with some of your camera's features will help you step up your photo-taking game!

Camera Basics

There are two basic ways of launching your camera app. One is as you would typically launch any app, by locating its app launch icon on one of your launch pages and tapping it. Your camera can also be launched from the lock screen. When you wake your phone from sleep mode, you will initially be directed to the launch screen, where you swipe or enter your preferred passcode to access your phone's contents. You can also access your camera from this screen, without having to unlock the phone. You will notice a small camera icon in the lower right-hand corner of your lock screen. Tap and drag upwards on this icon to launch your camera app. This is very useful for quickly capturing photo opportunities.

Your camera app will open with the rear-facing camera as its default device. The rear facing camera is on the back of your

Galaxy S5, pointing outwards, and is much higher resolution than your front-facing camera. As such, it is a good idea to use this camera whenever possible.

You will see the image currently being picked up by your camera on the screen. Move your S5 into position so that the image you would like to capture is in the correct position on your touchscreen. When you are ready to take the picture, tap the camera icon surrounded by the white circle, in the center at the bottom of your touchscreen. Your screen will flash very quickly and your picture will be taken.

In some instances and modes, you may need to hold your S5 in place for a bit longer while your image is captured. This is sometimes done if you want an enhanced image, or if you are shooting in a dark environment and your S5 needs to compensate for the lack of light. In this case, you will be prompted to do so by the text "Hold the device steady until it finishes taking the picture." You will see a blue line move around the camera circle. Hold the S5 still until your image is captured.

To view the photo you have just taken, as well as other captured images, tap the photo thumbnail, on the bottom left side of your touchscreen. Note that, if you opened your camera from the lock screen, and it is password protected, you will not be able to access other photos in your gallery, only take new photos. This is for your own security and protection. For more on photo and video options, see that section below.

Important Camera Functions

There are many important features that you can use to take better pictures using your S5 camera. Here, we discuss some of the most important features.

Front-facing Camera

The front facing camera is a lower-quality, 2-megapixel camera that is largely used for taking pictures of your own face, commonly known as "selfies." To change from the rear to front-facing camera, tap the icon of the camera with two arrows pointing opposite directions, on the top row of icons, all the way to the right. You should now see yourself, and the scene directly behind you. From this camera, you can take a photo or video in the typical way.

In some instances, your front-facing camera will also be automatically activated, for example, when you are video conferencing using your S5. This happens without you taking any additional action, and, in most cases, is not optional. That is, you *must* only use the front-facing camera for various types of video conferencing. When this occurs, you will not see the usual camera functions.

Note, too, that some of the other functions described below are not available for the front facing camera.

Camera focus circle

You will occasionally notice a circle that pops up in the center of your camera frame. It will rotate and zoom in quickly on the middle of your screen, then disappear. This is your camera's focus circle. You can use this circle to draw the center of focus of your S5's camera, for example, to make it focus on people's faces or the center of a painting.

To do so, tap once on the part of the frame where you would like to focus your camera. You can also tap and then hold and drag to determine the best spot to focus your camera. You should see the focus circle move with your finger, and then notice that the picture sharpens in that area. It takes some practice to become proficient with the focus circle, but it is well worth it.

Zoom functions

Your rear-facing camera is equipped with a very powerful zoom function that magnifies images up to four times (4x). To zoom in, tap and hold two of your fingers on the screen, then making a finger spreading gesture. You will see the camera begin to zoom in, and a white box will appear, above which you can see the number of times the image is magnified. To stop zooming in, merely take your fingers off the screen. After you have reached your desired zoom level, it is a good idea to refocus the camera again using the camera focus circle before taking your picture.

To zoom out, place two fingers on the screen again and make a pinching motion, or move your fingers in towards each other, such that they meet towards the center of the touchscreen. Your camera will stop zooming out once it has reached normal magnification again.

HDR

HDR is short for high-dynamic-range imaging. HDR is an advanced means of taking digital photos that provides for more verisimilitude in picture capture, but that takes up more memory space. HDR photos will especially show a greater contrast between light and dark areas in a photo.

To turn on HDR, tap the icon of the sun next to an empty circle, on the top row, second from the left, on your main camera's screen.

Selective focus

Selective focus is a function that allows you to take in-focus pictures of objects in the foreground, while the background will be distinctly out of focus. This is usually employed for artistic effect, but can have some practical uses as well. To toggle on the selective focus effect, tap the icon of the two figures enclosed by a bracket, third from the left on the top row of icons.

Camera Modes

You can select from among a number of camera modes. To access your mode options, tap the "Mode" icon, on the bottom icon row, between your gallery thumbnail and the camera icon. Below is a brief description of each mode. Note that some modes are only functional when using the rear-facing cameras, while others require you to use the front-facing camera, or both.

Auto – The default camera mode. The camera will focus automatically and only take one shot when the camera icon is tapped once. The camera will automatically convert to low-light mode when required.

Beauty face – Beauty face is a newer feature that effectively works as automatic airbrushing. Beauty face automatically smoothes out blemishes and wrinkles on people's faces. You can set it at different levels, with 1 being the least active and 5 being the most active. Note that the front-facing camera will automatically default to beauty mode. You can toggle beauty mode on and off by using the icon in the upper right hand corner. You can also increase or decrease its strength by tapping and dragging on this icon.

Shot and more – In shot and more mode, you can take multiple pictures by tapping the camera icon once. The S5 will then combine or collect these photos in different option categories, allowing you to do things like select the best photo from a series, or combine a series of photos into one action shot.

Panorama – Panorama mode allows you to take panoramic pictures by slowly moving your phone across an image that is larger than that which you can capture within your typical camera window. Select panorama mode then tap the camera icon once and slowly move your phone across the scene you wish to capture. Your S5 will generate a panoramic image.

Virtual tour – This mode allows you to create walkthroughs of your physical surroundings. Select this mode, then follow the onscreen instructions. You will be asked to center the screen, then walk forward, turning periodically to create your walkthrough. Make sure to use this mode in a space where you can proceed in a continuous, linear fashion, as retracing your steps will create errors with the final walkthrough that you generate.

Dual camera – Dual camera mode allows you to simultaneously capture a photo taken by the rear and front-facing cameras.

Enable this mode, then tap the camera icon once to take a photo from both cameras.

Download – Tap download to see other modes that are available for your camera to download. You can download these and incorporate them into your camera's mode repertoire.

Taking Video

To take a video instead of a photo, tap the video camera icon, on the bottom of your touchscreen, directly to the right of the camera icon. Once you tap the video icon, your video will start recording. You can pause the video mid-capture, by tapping the pause button, and restart by tapping the red record button again. Once you have finished taking your video, tap the white square stop button. Your video is now available in your gallery, along with your photos.

Accessing Photos and Videos

As mentioned above, you can access your main photos library from the camera app, by tapping the thumbnail images in the lower left corner. You can also access your photos by tapping on the Gallery icon, found on your launch pages.

When you launch your Gallery, you will see a scroll of all the photos and videos you have captured with your phone. You can arrange the way these media are grouped by tapping on the icon of three horizontal bars in the uppermost left hand corner of your phone. You will see the options to view photos arranged by time, that is least to most recent or by album, if you have grouped your photos into albums. To create a new album, simply tab the folder icon with the small plus, on the upper toolbar. You will be asked to name your album, then it will appear in a left-side toolbar. Drag and drop photos into the album to move them permanently to that album.

Here, you can also filter your media by event, people, and scenery. Your S5 will autodetect these features, and present them to you as per its own detections. Event is determined by the place where the photos were taken, which requires that you have location services turned on. Your S5 will autodetect photos that have "People" in them, and only show these kinds of photos.

Conversely, your S5 will display people-less shots, defined as "Scenery."

Media Editing Options

Editing Photos

The Galaxy S5 possesses some of the most advanced photo and video options available on a smartphone which, at times, rival those of some available on personal computers. To access some of these photo capabilities, first select a photo from the image gallery. Then, tap the options icon in the upper right hand corner. Some of the most useful options are described below:

Copy to clipboard – Copies the image so that you can paste it into messages to send.

Rotate left/right – Rotates the image 90 degrees in either direction.

Crop - Allows you to readjust the borders of the image.

Rename - Allows you to give the image a more recognizable name.

Slideshow - View all images within an album as a scroll.

Set as - Allows you to set the album as wallpaper, a contact avatar, or for your home and lock screen backgrounds.

Studio - The studio function is a whole world unto itself, essentially a high powered photo editing studio. Here you can browse effects, alter the image, and radically alter it, if you wish.

When you are done editing your photo, you can share it by tapping the link icon, three small circles connected by lines, at the top of the touchscreen, second from left. Your S5 will then present you with the sharing options. Tap your selection to share your photo.

Editing Videos

While your video editing options are not as advanced as your photo editing options, you are still afforded a fairly amount of flexibility in video editing. Select a video from your gallery, then tap the play button in the center of your touchscreen to review it. Note that you can advance and reverse the video by tapping and dragging the blue circle at the bottom of the touchscreen to the left and right.

To edit your video, tap the scissors icon at the top of your touchscreen. You will then be taken to the video trimmer. To trim the sides of the video, drag the silver tabs on the left and right side of the screen. These will adjust the start and stop times of the video. Note that you cannot edit from the middle of the video, only from the beginning and end. You can also rotate the video clip if you wish, by tapping "rotate" at the top of the screen. Once you are done editing your video, tap "done" in the upper right hand corner. You will then be asked to enter a file name, and your S5 will save the new file.

As with photos, you can share videos by tapping the share icon, on the upper row, directly to the left of the scissors. Select the mode by which you'd like to share the video and your S5 will upload it.

Taking Your Galaxy Further

While the descriptions above give some sense of the basic apps and functions you can use in your day-to-day interaction with your Galaxy S5, there are a host of apps and special features that make your Galaxy even more special. Some of the most unique and eye-popping are highlighted below.

Special Phone Features

This section covers built in features of your smartphone that don't necessitate using any third-party apps and are built into the phone.

Download Booster

Download booster is a feature whereby your Galaxy S5 will *combine* data streams from both Wi-Fi and your cellular data networks so that you can download content more quickly. Note that download booster only works when you are downloading content to your phone, not when you are using a streaming service, such as YouTube.

To turn on download booster, swipe down from the top of your screen to open your notifications center. Swipe through the top row icons until you reach the download booster. Tap the icon to turn on the download booster. You will now see the booster's activity in your notification window whenever you are downloading content.

Note that if you do not see the download booster in your notification function row, you should tape the graphic of the divided square, in the upper right hand corner of the notifications pane, to the left of the settings gear wheel. Here, you will see a list of all available function buttons. You can either turn on download booster at this screen, or, if you would like, make it a permanent fixture of your available function buttons. To complete the latter task, tap the pencil icon at the top of the screen. Then, tap and drag the download booster icon from beneath "available buttons" into a space under the heading "active buttons." You can perform this process for any notification panel button you'd like to swap into the function row.

Quick Connect

Quick connect is a great way to share files quickly over your local network. Also available from your notifications window, activate quick connect to view other users and devices sharing the same network as you. You can drag and drop media, text, and data files to other users on your network.

Activate quick connect via the same method described for *Download Booster*, above. Search in your notification function row, and, if you don't find it there, tap the icon in the uppermost right hand corner, next to the gear wheel. You can find your quick connect icon here, and transfer it to the function row by tapping the pencil icon and manually moving it, if you like.

Private Mode

Private mode is a feature that allows you to secure and hide personal content within your Galaxy S5. You can activate private mode for particular applications, especially those that allow you to take media or store personal files. This is useful for safeguarding particular files that you want to bar access to.

To activate private mode, again find its icon in your notification window, via the method described in the previous two sections. Tap the "private mode" to enable it, and then watch the brief introductory slide show. You will then be prompted to select a security mode, running the gamut from drawing a pattern to using your fingerprint as the unlock mechanism. Private mode will inform you which apps it has been enabled for.

Having enabled private mode, you can now place your personal content under private control. Navigate to one of the apps for which private mode has been enabled. Within the app's main screen, tap the Options icon, and then tap "select," available from most main options menus. You will then be able to tap on the objects, whether they are photos, files, or other media, that you would like to select. Once you have checked the objects you'd like to move to your private folder, tap the Options icon again, and select "Move to Private."

To retrieve items from your private folder, go to the master directory My Files (contained within your Apps folder). Tap My Files, and then access "Private," below the Local Storage heading. If you have not recently unlocked your phone, you will have to perform the unlock method to view this media.

Toolbox

Your toolbox is a convenient way to add more app launch capability to your launch pages without having to change the structure of those pages. By enabling the toolbox, you can activate a convenient, very small widget that stores app icons to a few oft-used apps that you were not able to fit on your primary shortcut row.

To enable the toolbox, again navigate to the notification function row, using the above method described to locate the Toolbox activation button, if necessary. Once you have located the Toolbox icon, tap it once to activate it.

You should now see an opaque white circle with three dots in the middle, somewhere on the upper right-hand side of your S5's screen. Tapping this icon once will reveal the apps located in your toolbox. They default to: camera, Internet, voice recorder, memo, and calculator. You can tap any of these icons to launch that app. Tapping the white Toolbox circle again will hide these items.

Note that you can tap on and drag the white Toolbox circle to any location on your screen, without interfering with the layout of that launch page. If you would like to change the apps nested in the Toolbox, tap and hold on the Toolbox icon. You will see an option to Edit, with a pencil icon, appear on the upper left hand side of your screen. Drag the Toolbox icon here and release it. You will then be able to select from available apps by tapping on the check boxes to the right of the app's name. If you would like to remove the toolbox from your screen, tap and drag it to the upper right hand corner, where you will see the trashcan icon and the Remove text.

Using Gestures

Your Galaxy S5 comes with the capability to respond to gestures you make in front of the phone's touchscreen, without actually touching the phone. While some are more reliable than others, using gestures can greatly enhance your phone experience.

To activate gestures, swipe down on any screen to enter the notifications pane. Select the "Controls" category by swiping among the top categories. Here, you should see the "Motion" category. Tap on "Motions and gestures" to view the available gesture controls. They are as follows:

Air browse: Allows you to scroll between pages and lists by passing the knife-edge of your hand across the screen without touching it. At this page, you can set your preferences for which items you would like to manipulate via air browse.

Direct call: Activating direct call allows you to answer calls directly by moving the Galaxy S5 into position in front of your ear. This can be a very convenient way of answering your phone without having to touch or look at the screen.

Smart alert: Smart alert will send a notification to you when you pick your phone up after having left it on a flat surface for a period of time. You will be notified of any calls or messages you have missed in the interim.

Mute/pause: Mute/pause functionality allows you to mute calls or pause video on your screen by covering the screen with your hand, or by turning your phone over such that its touchscreen is facing down. You can control which gestures will enable mute pause in the settings menu at this screen.

Palm swipe to capture: This feature allows you to capture an image of the screen by swiping the knife-edge of your hand all the way from one side of the touchscreen to the other. This is a useful way of capturing screen shots of your phone's screen.

Air View

Air view is a functional cousin of Gestures, that allows you to interact with your phone without actually touching the screen. When air view is enabled, you can view calendar events, photos, speed dial information, and track through videos you are watching, merely by hovering your finger over the screen. Using air view can accelerate your interaction with your Galaxy S5.

Featured Apps and Widgets

Beyond your Galaxy S5's built in functionality there are many apps built specifically for the S5 that offer incredible features and functionality, and are must-haves for your Galaxy S5. There are many hundreds of fantastic apps for your Galaxy S5, but some of the very best are highlighted below. Some of these apps come preloaded, and others require a download from the Google Play store.

Smart Remote

One of the most lauded and discussed features of the Galaxy S5, smart remote is a universal remote controller that can be used to control any TV, and many other devices. This app comes preloaded on your Galaxy S5 and can be accessed via your Apps folder.

The smart remote requires a bit of initial setup, but it is well worth taking the time to do so. You will first be prompted to enter some information about your local cable provider, address, and your TV make and model.

You will then need to allow the phone to complete a process where it finds the appropriate signals to send to your TV to allow it to act as a remote controller. This could take some time, but just remember to keep a clear path between the TV and your S5 and not to move the phone around too much.

After your S5 determines the correct signals for your TV, you will be able to name your profile (e.g., after the location of your TV) and begin controlling your TV from your S5.

If you would like to add additional profiles, you can do so by tapping the Settings arrow, in the upper right hand corner of your remote, and tapping "Add Room."

You should now be able to use the vast majority of the controls which your regular TV remote provides via your Galaxy S5.

S Health

S Health is the Galaxy S5's personal trainer app. It helps you manage health goals, and performs a host of other special functions.

Your S Health defaults to appear as a widget on one of your launch pages. If it does not appear here, it can be found in your main widgets menu, accessed via the Add Launch Page screen, after tapping the "Widgets" icon.

When you startup the S Health app you will be prompted to add basic information about yourself to help the app assess your health goals and current health. You will also have the option of logging into your Samsung account to share your data with other S Health users and monitor your health achievements.

When you access the main screen, you will see that your S Health app has an integrated suite of health-oriented trackers to help you stay in touch with your health goals. Using these functions in concert is the best way to get the most out of this app:

Pedometer – Track how many steps you take per day. You can set goals for yourself and track your progress, accessible via the green bar graph icon in the lower left-hand corner.

Exercise – Log your exercise routines, including the type of activity, your location, and how many calories you burn. The S5 will also compile data on your daily workouts.

Heart Rate – Measure your heart rate periodically throughout the day. Active the heart rate monitor, then place your finger over your camera flash on the back of the S5, as prompted by the Galaxy. Your S5 will measure your heart rate and log it so that you can check on your changing heart rate.

Food - Accessible via the menu bars in the upper left hand corner of the main screen, use the food app to log your diet everyday. This way, the S5 can show you how efficiently you burn calories that you consume, and how healthy your diet is.

There are more apps available for S Health, but, for the fitness-minded, it is an incredibly useful app.

Drive Mode

Drive Mode is a feature which automatically blocks incoming calls and texts when your phone is traveling at driving speeds. This app is developed specifically for stopping texting and driving-related accidents.

The app should be accessible via your main Apps folder. Once opening the app, you will have the opportunity to set your Drive Mode preferences. These include a number of useful features:

AutoReply: Autoreply will automatically send a text to contacts who call or text you while Drive Mode is enabled. This is perfect for letting your contacts know that you are driving and will call when you have the opportunity. You can toggle autoreply on and off in your Drive Mode settings. You can also set an "AutoReply Message," that your contacts will receive when they try to call or text you.

Allow List: You can add contacts to your allow list to let their communication come through, even when you are driving.

Automatic Mode: Leaving automatic mode enabled means that your Drive Mode will automatically activate when your S5 detects that it is traveling faster than twenty-five miles per hour. If you leave this feature disabled, you must manually turn on drive mode every time you begin driving.

Parental Alerts: This function will allow Drive Mode to text another number (presumably a parent contact number) if Drive Mode is disabled for any reason. Parental Alerts are password controlled, and so cannot be disabled, except by using the password.

Kids Mode

Kids Mode is a great feature that essentially renders your S5 child friendly. The app is available from the Google Play store, and does not come preloaded on your phone. Once you have downloaded and installed the app, you can install the widget on your launch screen, or simply launch the app from its icon.

The first time you start up Kids Mode, you will be required to enter a PIN. This is to ensure that your child is unable to access the rest of the phone without entering your PIN. Once you have entered Kids Mode, a number of child-friendly apps will become available. These mirror the features of the S5 in many ways, but are developed specifically for children.

To exit Kids Mode, tap the icon of the exit door on the Kids Mode main screen, in the lower right hand corner. You will need to re-enter your PIN at this point.

The Google Suite of Apps

As mentioned above, you must log into the S5 on initial setup using your Google account. While this is all that's absolutely necessary, familiarizing yourself with the Google suite of apps is highly recommended. As the Android operating system is developed in close consultation with Google product development, these apps often integrate seamlessly into use with the Galaxy S5. Some of the more useful Google apps are highlighted below.

Most of your Google Apps can be found nested in the "Google" folder, which will default as an icon on one of your launch pages. They can also be found individually within your Apps folder.

Google Chrome – Google's flagship Internet browser application. Google Chrome is an extremely lightweight browser that will put minimal memory drag on your S5 while providing everything you would expect from a mobile Internet browser. Maybe of the instructions which apply to the S5's native Internet browser (described above) also apply to Google Chrome, as the Internet browser is closely modeled on Chrome. One major advantage of using Google Chrome on your Galaxy S5 is its ability to transfer your Chrome windows to any desktop or laptop computer also running Chrome under your Google account. That is, if you have certain windows open in your mobile Chrome browser on your S5, you can easily access these on your home computer as well. This provides for seamless Internet browsing, whether on the go or at home.

Gmail – Google's email app will already be familiar to the many millions of users who use it in its desktop incarnation. One of the major advantages to using Gmail is its category-based filing that automatically filters messages into a number of preset categories, allowing you to keep clear partitions between your different types of email. Adding secondary accounts with Gmail is also very easy. Gmail, however, is a bit slower to search your inbox than the S5's native client, and so, is a bit of a toss-up in terms of advantages between the two. As with Chrome and the S5's native Internet, the controls for using Gmail are very similar to the native Email app.

Google Drive – Google's cloud storage app is a great way to transfer files and access your cloud-based data and spreadsheets. Your S5 is designed to contribute to your Drive, not just be a reader for it, and, as such, you can scan images, create new Google Drive files, and upload material from your phone to your Google Drive. Using Drive routinely is probably one of the surest ways to guarantee an easy flow of files between your personal computer and your S5.

Google Maps – Google's navigation and maps service is one of the best and most robust on the market. When you are signed in to your Google account, Maps will save previously visited addresses and locations, making it easy to get to some of your favorite places with a few taps. Google Maps also possesses a GPS navigation feature that will work just as an independent GPS navigation unit. You can find directions for walking, biking, driving, and using public transportation.

Hangouts – Google Hangouts are a great way to teleconference with people, or just to catch up with friends. Hangouts is one of the apps to take advantage of your front facing camera, and, via wireless network, presents one of the most advanced mobile video conferencing experiences to date. The S5's large display is perfect for this sort of activity, and you will find that using Google Hangouts on your smartphone is nearly as enjoyable as on your personal computer. Hangouts can support multiple users at once, and is perfect for quickly engaging in group conferencing.

Backup & Restore

Another feature of being synchronized with your Google account is the ability to backup your S5's data. Selecting this option will ensure that your Galaxy S5 continually updates information from your phone to your Google account. Typical backup information includes your personal settings, apps on your phone, and information like bookmarks and Wi-Fi passwords. If you ever lose the data on your phone, or wish to reset it, you can always restore from data that has been backed up via this function.

If your phone should ever crash for any reason, you will be able to restore much of the data from your Google backup. You can toggle this option on and off in your settings menu, accessed via your notification center, under "General" and in the "Backup and reset" category. Make sure that "Back up my data" is checked off. Google will automatically receive backups of your S5's data, periodically.

Transferring Files

You may want to transfer files from your computer to your Galaxy S5. One of the fastest ways to do so may be to upload items to an application, such as Google Drive, but you can also transfer files manually, via USB cable or your local network connection.

Android File Transfer, available from the Android site, is the preferred solution for USB cable transfers. You can download and install the application on your computer, then attach the provided USB cable to your computer to manually move files via USB. This is a much more secure option that moving items over the network, and may be preferred when moving sensitive data.

Another fantastic means of remotely controlling and updating your S5 is Airdroid, available from www.airdroid.com. While Airdroid will transfer files via your network, not USB cable, it is a direct transfer, without an intermediary step of uploading those files to a cloud server. Airdroid also allows you to perform functions such as texting from your personal computer, which can be very convenient. Airdroid will also allow you to deactivate a lost or stolen phone remotely, which provides the user with a great deal of security.

Accessories

There are a number of accessories available for you Galaxy S5 on the market. Some of the best and most essential are listed below.

S5 Phone Case – A phone case is essential to protect your S5 against drops, spills and other mishaps. When looking for a case, make sure to get something that is durable, while not greatly increasing the dimensions of the phone. Some of the best cases are made by Speck, Urban Armor, and Spigen.

Screen Protector – A good screen protector will keep dust, grime, and water off of your phone's display screen, increasing its life and functionality. The ideal screen protector is thin and nearly invisible, but durable and resistant to the elements. Tech Armor andBody Guardz both make good screen protectors.

Bluetooth Headset – A Bluetooth headset is a great way to wirelessly communicate via your Galaxy S5 without having to pick up your phone. Ensure that you find a headset that is lightweight and comfortable for you to wear, such that you can leave it in for prolonged periods of time. Also check, of course, that the headset is compatible with the Galaxy S5. NoiseHush makes a great compact and stylish Bluetooth headset that is compatible, as does Platronics.

Charging Cradles and Docks – Charging cradles and docks are great homes for you Galaxy S5 when you are not using it. These ensure that your photo keeps its charge, and is always easy to find. These are also very useful for holding your phone in position for long teleconferencing sessions or speakerphone or Bluetooth calls.

Troubleshooting

Some brief tips for troubleshooting common problems and solving common issues with the S5 are included here. As the S5 is a very complicated device, a host of issues can arise, but this guide covers some quick fixes.

Galaxy S5 Will Not Turn On

If your S5 does not turn on, the most likely issue is a lack of battery power. Connect the phone to its charger and leave it for an hour or so to gain some initial charge. If the phone's battery is completely dead it may not be able to turn on for some time, even when connected to a power source. It should regain initial charge after a bit and you will be able to turn it on.

Galaxy S5 Displays Network Error Messages

The most likely cause of this is that your S5 is unable to access the network. Check the status bar to make sure you have mobile service, indicated by the service bars. Also check to see that your Wi-Fi is working properly, if connected. Keep in mind that your phone will occasionally encounter dead service spots, and that this is normal.

S5 Does Not Send or Receive Text Messages

If you transferred from an iPhone device to your S5, the iMessage function on your iPhone might be trapping all text communication, if still activated. Return to your old iPhone, enter the settings menu, and locate iMessage. Tap the icon next to iMessage once to deactivate it. You will need to perform this fix for all Apple devices that are iMessage enabled.

Galaxy Crashes Repeatedly or Displays Fatal Errors

You will likely have to reset your phone to factory defaults. Enter the notification center menu, navigate to the General category, and tap "backup and reset." At the bottom of the page, tap "Factory data reset." Remember that you will lose all your data when you complete this step, so ensure that you have backed it up.

Multimedia Files Will Not Open or S5 Will Not Save New Files

You have likely run out of media storage space on your S5. Delete some files, or transfer them to your desktop computer, and then delete them from your S5. You will need to make more room for multimedia files on your phone.

www.ingramcontent.com/pod-product-compliance
Lightning Source LLC
LaVergne TN
LVHW022349060326
832902LV00022B/4338